The Pleasures of Language:
From Acropox to Word Clay

Skip Eisiminger

Serving House Books

The Pleasures of Language:
From Acropox to Word Clay

ISBN: 978-0-9971010-9-6

Serving House Books logo by Barry Lereng Wilmont

Cover painting: Rotari, Pietro Antonio, Italian, 1707-1762
"Young Girl Writing a Love Letter," c. 1755
Oil on canvas, 33-3/8 x 27 in. (84.8 x 68.6 cm)
Norton Simon Art Foundation

Author photo by Ingrid Eisiminger

Published by Serving House Books, LLC
Copenhagen, Denmark and Florham Park, NJ

www.servinghousebooks.com

Member of the Independent Book Publishers Association

First Serving House Books Edition 2016

"Mark Twain defined wit as 'the sudden marriage of ideas which, before their union, were not perceived to have any relation,' and it is wit's investigation of various and sundry (and conjunction of hilarious and wondry) which makes the clever, word-infatuated, universe-ranging writing of Skip Eisiminger such a lasting delight." –Elizabeth Boleman-Herring, Editor, *Weekly Hubris*

"With seriously funny humor, profound insight and a vast accumulation of knowledge about '*words, words, words*' (their origins and flexibilities), Skip Eisiminger creates a world-class collection of beguiling essays investigating 'The richness (and rankness) of our language and the endless variations we weave with the muscles of our mouths [which] never grow tired of studying it.' From 'Acronym abuse' to 'Advertising Hullabaloo' to 'The Language of Sex' or the definitions of 'Tautologies,' *The Pleasures of Language* frames what is, in effect, a cornucopia of word-spinning meditations exploring the inexhaustible and continually evolving nature of human discourse." –Duff Brenna, Editor *Serving House Journal*

"Damn you, Eisiminger! I came to my office on my day off, with no students to meet, to get a jump on the endless grading and administrivia of my life, and instead I opened this book. Now, it's three hours later, I haven't graded a single paper, and all I've done is enjoy the company and wit of the Wordspinner!" –Chris Benson, Senior Lecturer in English

"Professor Eisiminger's labyrinth of evocative material reminds one of the imagination of P.T. Barnum. These essays are as singular in their intriguing variety as those of the master essayist E. B. White. They range from the literary to the everyman, sprinting from afternoon delights to an evening of fireside solemnity. Skipping (Skip) along from the Greeks, the Old Testament, to James Dickey the reader is cavorted through grammar to fickle students. These challenging essays are guaranteed to stimulate, guaranteed to question the reader—who, where, and what a treat!

No Hobsonian choice here, but a spiraling eclectic adventure."
–David Tillinghast, Professor Emeritus of English

"What do you do when you run across a word or phrase you don't know, say "balaclava," or "playing the dozens"? Do you find a dictionary and look it up, or do you blink your eyes and go on? If you are lucky, as I was for years, all I had to do was to step down the hall and ask "The Wordspinner" what a name such as "The Mull of Kintyre" was all about, and nine times out of ten he would give me both the meaning and the etymology of the term. The Wordspinner, known widely in print and by reputation, is Skip Eisiminger, a scholar who loves words. More than anyone I know of, Skip delights in the word. He is fascinated by its sound, shape, and promise of every word he sees. To him, as it was with Emily Dickinson, every word is a poem in itself. Not only does he cherish words, but he also published dozens of articles and books on this subject. At the next opportunity, I intend to ask him what "amphisbaena" is, a word I just can't bring myself to look up." –Harold Woodell, Professor Emeritus of English

"Skip is able to weave personal experiences, historical events, and interesting tidbits into each of his pieces with such finesse and poise that one cannot help but be engrossed by the final product. Coupled with his expert handling of language and deep reservoir of knowledge, his work is something to be both admired and studied by writers and scholars alike." –Brennan Beck, Assistant Director Military and Veteran Engagement, Clemson University

"These essays by Skip Eisiminger are not only engaging and contain material that I had never thought of before; but, in addition, they often address important topics in a very important way." –Ronald Moran, Professor Emeritus of English and Associate Dean

To Anja, Brook, Aimee, and Shane—love you guys.

Books by Skip Eisiminger

Wordspinner (Rowman and Littlefield, 1991)

Felix Academicus: Tales of a Happy Academic (Clemson University Digital Press, 2007)

Letters to the Grandchildren (Clemson University Press, 2010)

Acknowledgments

The author would like to thank Wayne Chapman of *The South Carolina Review*, Duff Brenna of the *Serving House Journal*, Clare MacQueen of *KYSO Flash*, Robert H. Fiske of *Vocabula*, and Elizabeth Boleman-Herring of *Weekly Hubris* for their long-standing support and kindness.

Contents

Introduction

I don't recall the numbers, but in the tenth grade, my verbal score on the P-SAT disappointed my father even though it was better than my math score, so he bought me a pocket dictionary and told me to place a check mark next to every word I looked up. If I looked up a word more than once, he said, I was to chop off a finger. He was kidding, of course, but that small leather-bound book that smelled of the Pentagon branch of Brentano's, and the crosswords I began doing in *The Stars and Stripes* during my army enlistment were the beginnings of my formal and informal study of words—among my first experiences with the pleasures of language.

At Auburn, I took a history of the language class from Dr. Leo Gosser, one of the editors of *A Dictionary of Americanisms on Historical Principles* (1951). He, perhaps more than any, showed me the beckoning backdoor of English (slang, dialect, euphemisms, etc.), and I burst in like a thirsty boozehound during Prohibition.

At Clemson, when Col. Ben Skardon, coiner of "suslavatism," retired, I was offered English 217, Vocabulary Building, and I grabbed it like those Minoan youths who somersaulted over the horns of a charging bull. I taught one section of that course most semesters for twenty years before I gathered some of my materials and discovered that Rowman and Littlefield was willing to publish the book that became *Wordspinner* in 1991.

Since retiring from Clemson in 2010, I've taught four, ten-week "Pleasures of Language" classes at the local Osher Lifelong Learning Institute. My wife, students, and friends have often threatened me with an "intervention," and perhaps I need one, but if I die like Yeats with a book in my hands, you'll know I died happy.

"Suslavatism," incidentally, is neo-Latin for "hogwash," and I trust you won't find any examples of it from my keyboard in the following pages. If you do, I'll move to Texas and help Donald Trump build "the Great Wall of America," which of course, is suslavatism.

—Skip Eisiminger

Acropox: Acronyms

"The French spell NATO backwards but pronounce it forwards."—
The Wordspinner

"If FEDEX and UPS were to merge, would they call it FED
UP?"—*Anonymous*

In 1950, Fred Iacocca chose not to bestow a "junior" on his
son, Ed, but perhaps he should have. Fred was named by
his father, Luigi, who had joined FIGHT REDS, EXPAND
DEMOCRACY, which was long before ERECTILE
DYSFUNCTION shriveled into ED. Ed's mother, Jan,
had approved the name because, as she told friends, "I'm
JUST A NURSE," and she was. However, to her patients,
she was the woman with the MILK OF MAGNESIA; to
Fred, she was the MASTER OF MAGIC, and to Ed, she
was the MAKER OF ME.

When Fred's second cousin took over at Chrysler
years later, Jan said it was clear he was perfect for the job
given that "Iacocca" stood for "I AM CHAIRMAN OF
CHRYSLER CORPORATION OF AMERICA." (To
Ed, however, Fred was "Dad," the DEPUTY ASSISTANT
DIRECTOR of something slightly less ambiguous than
his title.) However, Fred, who'd always driven Fords, was
torn by his cousin's success. He favored Fords because they
were FIRST ON RACE DAY, but Jan, who loved the
Dodge, countered with her own etymology: FOUND ON
ROAD DEAD. Fred was ready for her, however, claiming
that Dodges were DEAD ON DAY GUARANTEE
EXPIRES.

By the time Ed learned to drive, he had all the
symptoms of his parents' acronymic disorder. For example,
he had difficulty remembering whether "stop" stood for

11

SLIGHT TOUCH OF PEDAL, or, SPIN TIRES ON PAVEMENT. Nor could he recall if "kiss" meant KEEP IT SHORT [and] SWEET, … SIMPLE [and] SAFE, or … SLOPPY [and] SEXY. Despite Jan's efforts to educate her son sexually from autoeroticism to zooerasty, Ed was not her best student: for years, he did not understand why the NCAA forced the Friends' University Christian Knights to change their mascot's name, and he was thirty before he understood that "gay" did not imply the following question: GOT AIDS YET? Jan assigned her son's lapses to "acropox."

For Ed, the problem of reading a new acronym or initialism was the same as "reading" an inkblot. Was IHOP the INTERNATIONAL HOUSE OF PANCAKES or the INVENTORY [of] HAZARDOUS OP[erations]? And couldn't IHOP have been INTERPAN or INHOUSECAKES? It all seemed so arbitrary.

His disorder worsened in high school when he took a history class from Mr. Otto Hannah. Palindromic Hannah, who'd failed the language-history course at TriBeCa Tech, informed the class that "wop" was an Italian immigrant WITHOUT PAPERS, "tip" originated from the custom of leaving coins for a server TO INSURE PROMPTNESS, "news" derived from NORTH EAST WEST SOUTH, and the first "cop" was a CONSTABLE ON PATROL." Ed started calling the school's folk etymologist "Mr. Emota," short for, EXPLAIN MEANING OF THE ACRONYM.

Hannah, who'd urged his class to read the Bible because it contained BASIC INFORMATION BEFORE LEAVING EARTH, shocked everyone when he announced his resignation. It seems the police had sent him and dozens of others a letter claiming to be from the

JOINT AMERICAN INHERITANCE LOCATORS. Thirty others with outstanding warrants swallowed the bait. Red-faced, he told the class he'd overlooked the letterhead clue since "jail" was spelled "g-a-o-l" at Tech.

The superintendent replaced Hannah with a woman who taught a course called, "A History of WEIRD Countries" in the sense of WESTERN, EDUCATED, INDUSTRIALIZED, RICH, [and] DEMOCRATIC [Countries]. Ed was delighted to learn that the Navy had all but invited the Japanese to "sink us" in WWII. Not until after Pearl Harbor did CINCUS, the COMMANDER IN CHIEF [of the] US [Navy], edit his titular nomenclature.

After graduation, Ed enlisted in the army, which, as far as he could tell, had never invited an enemy to bomb us. As luck would have it, he was sent to a Ranger battalion whose motto was TESTICLES: TEAMWORK, ENTHUSIASM, STAMINA, TENACITY, INITIATIVE, COURAGE, LOYALTY, EXCELLENCE, [and a] SENSE [of humor]. Most of his buddies thought the motto was too long, but Ed loved it. However, he found himself in hot water when he began placing his own stamp on the army's acronyms. When the operation, code-named IOWA, began, Ed explained that the men on maneuvers were IDIOTS OUT WALKING AROUND. The colonel, a Hawkeye, was not amused.

After his tour was up, Ed took the test for MENSA but qualified for DENSA, an organization for those DIVERSELY EDUCATED, [but] NOT SERIOUSLY AFFECTED by the experience. He tried joining the Mormons, but when he learned that LDS did not stand for LAY DOWN, SISTER, he turned to alcohol.

In the COYOTE (CUT OUT YOUR OLD TIRED ETHICS) Bar one night, he met Meg, a woman with

BITCH embroidered across the back of her jacket. Ed was smitten when he learned that she was a BROAD IN TOTAL CONTROL [of] HERSELF. Meg in turn was taken by this SENSITIVE NEW AGE GUY who had SNAG tattooed on his forearm. But when she told Ed about her work with MADD: MOTHERS AGAINST DRUNK DRIVERS, he panicked and joined DAMM: DRUNKS AGAINST MAD MOTHERS.

At TriBeCa Tech where Ed was now enrolled, an organization named BACCHUS (BOOST ALCOHOL CONSCIOUSNESS CONCERNING [the] HEALTH [of] UNIVERSITY STUDENTS) helped our protagonist dry out, but the mixed message conveyed by the name sent Ed to CADAVER. This was a campus club made up of CHRISTIANS AGAINST DRUGS AND VIOLENCE [and for] EQUAL RIGHTS, but again there was that unsettling message in the name.

His parents, meanwhile, had joined a fundamentalist mission named MOM, which stood for MARY, OUR MOTHER. MOM was run by Father Jim, a defrocked priest, who claimed that "Jim" stood for JESUS IN ME. His favorite Bible verse was even less inclusive; it was simply TGIF: THANK GOD I'M FORGIVEN. Nevertheless, his take on SIN (SELF-INFLICTED NONSENSE) and EGO (EDGING GOD OUT) appealed to Ed. But when the collection plate made the rounds on Sunday, it was "Hail, Mary and get out the CASH," for CHRISTIANS ALWAYS SAY HALLELUJAH in Father Jim's church. Jim explained that God wanted his people to go first-class, and since Jaguar could only mean JESUS ALWAYS GUIDES US AND REDEEMS, Jim drove one.

Though Fred and Jan remained with the padre hoping to trade up to a Jaguar, Ed had had his fill. He founded AAAAAA: the AMERICAN ASSOCIATION AGAINST ACRONYM ABUSE ANONYMOUS, had a tattoo removed, married Meg, and got on with his life.

At last sighting, Ed was driving a Ford and stopping at most intersections.

Infinitum: Advertising

"Advertising: hullabaloo; speculation and a mad dash for profits have made advertising a means of swindling the people and of foisting upon them goods frequently useless or of dubious quality."
—*Great Soviet Encyclopedia, 1941 edition*

"Advertising: the popularization of goods with the aim of selling them; the creation of demand for these goods." —*Great Soviet Encyclopedia, 2014 edition*

Born in 1941, I grew up with the jingles on Mother's kitchen radio like: "My beer is Rheingold, the dry beer; think of Rheingold whenever you buy beer!" In the 1950s, traveling between Virginia and Georgia, my sisters and I would vie for the right to read aloud the next set of Burma Shave signs: "Said Farmer Brown / who's bald on top / wish I could / rotate the crop. / Burma Shave!" In high school, a young friend thought I was the bees' knees because I delivered *The Washington Post* for the man who drew the Coppertone ad showing a girl's bare bottom. That passed for sex in the 1950s. And finally, seduced by posters of Bavaria, I enlisted in the army because the recruiters promised to send me to Germany. Technically, they upheld their end of the bargain, but I was stationed four hundred miles north of the Alps in a Wehrmacht ammunition factory on "Gallows Hill" for most of my enlistment. Winter in Germany had looked a lot cooler on the posters; Heidwinkel/Bahrdorf was just cold.

All-day suckers such as my younger self are what cartoonist Robert Mankoff was aiming at when he drew a consumer at a cigarette kiosk asking the clerk, "Oh, just give me a pack of whatever the guys in marketing are targeting for jerks like me." Mankoff's colleague at the *New*

Yorker Jack Ziegler gives the ad maker his comeuppance at a chaotic press conference where he's explaining, "Yes, but take away the rodent droppings and the occasional shard of glass, and you've got a damn fine product." Somewhere between that ad man and the consumer lies a multi-billion-dollar industry.

Mostly, however, I come not to bury Little Caesars Pizza! Pizza! but to praise it. From Egyptian ads on papyrus flacking rewards for runaway slaves, advertising proved itself useful to those who could afford it in 2000 BC. Here's some more recent evidence of its success: in the 1930s, when the cartoon figure Popeye began eating spinach to increase his strength, sales of the vegetable soared 33%. Said Popeye, "I is strong to the finish / 'cause I eats me spinach." But spinach farmers were paying nothing for this product placement in the nation's newspapers, so King Features accepted the sponsorship of Wheatena breakfast cereal at $1,200 per week, and soon Popeye was singing, "Wheatena's me diet—I ax ya to try it." Meanwhile, spinach consumption held steady.

Judging by the two epigraphs above, advertising, this public service with a profit motive, has worked in most places including non-capitalist states like the former Soviet Union and countries like Japan which were late coming to capitalism. In 1959, it was a rare Japanese bride who received a diamond engagement ring. In the early 1960s, DeBeers, seeing a compact, untapped market of millions, began advertising in the Japanese media. Today, over 60% of Japanese brides are receiving diamonds, a percentage second only to the US.

Further evidence includes this research reported in *Harper's*: when the image of Elmo, the popular Sesame Street character, was pasted on cafeteria apples in 2012, consumption among elementary-school children rose 68%. It's a little like hiring a pretty, young actress to shill life insurance to the elderly. Nevertheless, "Doing business without advertising," wrote Stuart Britt, "is like winking at a girl in the dark. You know what you're doing, but nobody else does." I would add that if advertising didn't work, generic brands would be in short supply; they aren't.

Former madman-adman James Dickey told a poetry class at the University of South Carolina that when he worked in advertising he would "sell his soul during the day, and buy it back writing poetry at night." Ultimately, he was fired because he was investing more time in "purchasing" than marketing. With or without a soul, he was a master marketer, and I learned much observing him promote his work, so he could afford to write poetry on his six-figure salary.

Dickey also told his class that the worst ad he'd ever stumbled on was one published in the *Dublin News* in 1871. His agency agreed and made the advert available to its staff as a cautionary tale. It reads in part: "House to let...free from opacity, tenebrosity, fumidity, and injucundity—in short, its diaphaneity even in the crepuscule makes it like a Pharos...." After consulting the *Oxford English Dictionary*, I determined that this rental was clean with big windows.

If that Dublin to-let ad represents the over-stuffed *wurst* of questionable intent and origins, here are the standards which lead me to "turn toward" (the Latin sense of "advertise") any product vying for my attention. First is honesty. I know of no better example of this virtue than this ad (*circa*. 1860) for Pony Express riders: "Wanted: Young, skinny, wiry fellows, not over eighteen. Must be expert riders willing to risk death daily. Orphans preferred...." It reminds one of the ads (*circa*. 1900) seeking volunteers for polar expeditions, "...safe return doubtful."

The second standard is understatement: "Rolls-Royce: the horsepower is adequate." Claiming that the Phantom model's V12 engine produced 453 horsepower surely would have been perceived as bluster in the House of Lords even if it was the truth.

Third is cleverness or subtlety as illustrated by the Justerini and Brooks Scotch Whisky ad: "ingle ells, ingle ells. The holidays aren't the same without J&B."

Fourth is humor as illustrated by this Sunsweet Pitted Prune ad: "Today the pits; tomorrow the wrinkles." The only reason there isn't more humor in ads is that it's so hard to write, and gifted comics like Stan Freberg, who wrote this one, are so rare.

Fifth is closely related to humor: wit. "Haul derrière," a Mercedes slogan, had it. So did VW's counter-culture claim, "Kick asphalt."

Radio ads get a bye in my final category: visual interest. My favorite here is an ad for a "burn plaster" sold by the German firm Hansaplast showing a shirtless rocker diving into a sea of flaming cigarette lighters. I could neither watch the complete ad nor look away.

Naked hucksterism, "Buy this, you idiot," may open more wallets, but for many consumers, there's the reverse-psychology factor to consider. Take the Charmin toilet paper slogan, "Enjoy the go." The subtext is "buy me," but many hear only a flush.

⁂

Consumers must always beware the large print which giveth and the fast talking which taketh away, but advertising has come a long way in four thousand years as has humanity. For one thing, we no longer advertise for runaway slaves. And thanks to government, we no longer have to worry whether Fruitcura cough medicine is 40% alcohol, or if smoking Kool cigarettes will cure that cough, or if the bikini marked "50% off" comes without a top.

We still need to make sure we're focused on the champagne, not the bubbles, because the dynamic ingredient in most offers remains marketing. Are we buying a Big Ass fan because of its reliability or its hip name and the horse's-ass logo? Indeed, Asics kneepads are $4 more with the logo than without. I once bought an Omega wristwatch in part because it had a "jeweled movement." Then I learned that the sapphires are synthetic and cost a nickel apiece, less than the steel they replaced.

Peeing in a Pool Because It's Kidney Shaped: Analogies

"All perception of truth is the perception of analogy; we reason from our hands to our head." —*Henry David Thoreau*

"All of us get our thoughts entangled in metaphors and act fatally on the strength of them." —*George Eliot*

Humankind's first analogies are forever lost, but there's a fair chance the tropes began when some cave dweller spotted a woolly mammoth browsing in a Provencal meadow and then sketched one in charcoal over his fireplace. "Surely," he thought, "there's a connection." Judging by the cave art in Southern Europe, by the time of the agricultural revolution 10,000 years ago, such analogies and sympathetic magic must have been commonplace.

Some anthropologists think that male circumcisions began when someone noticed that vines were more productive the year after they were cut back. "If pruning worked for the vine," thought the Cro-Magnon vintner, "why not my son's penis?" To this day, there are farmers who jump up and down or have intercourse in the fields to "insure" the harvest. Seductively persuasive as these practices are, once they get started, they are difficult to stop even if they work only 5% of the time. If the ritual fails, the witch doctor can always find an explanation in the "fine print."

In most Western circles until about 1600 AD, clever but non-rational analogies continued to be more persuasive than empirical science. For close to two thousand years, the brightest minds figured: if there are four seasons and elements, the body must have four humors or fluids. And if Aristotle thought of it first, it usually had the church's backing which guaranteed its longevity. Anonymous churchmen mused, "If there are seven planets, there surely are seven sins and seven virtues." The prospect of locating them was intoxicating, and the resulting correspondence was perfect, of course, as Aristotle predicted.

The misuse of analogies may be illustrated by Hitler's choice of the word "vermin" to argue for the persecution of the Jewish people. With the sanction of the country's elected leaders, Jews were publicly exposed in the Nazi's "antiseptic searchlight" as "rodents" deserving of nothing more than "disinfection." Many Germans without a record of violence then concluded that there was no reason to share the "harvest" with a subhuman species posing a threat to the commonweal, and with few exceptions they didn't.

Almost a century later, some us know better. We know that on one level the metaphor is always wrong—war is not hell, Jews are not vermin, nor is love located in heaven. Our enemies have no horns, Jews are human beings with inalienable rights, and love is right here—always has been.

Which is not to say that analogies are useless. When a home-heating engineer explained to my wife and me why our heat pump had quit five years after its installation, he said, "Your system has worn itself out like someone sucking on a crimped straw. Next time you drink a milk shake," he advised, "pinch the straw, suck hard, and you'll soon feel the muscles in your cheeks ache." Both of us understood immediately that our air-intake duct needed to be enlarged. Likewise, when my urologist finished a digital examination, he said with a sigh, "This is like estimating the height of the Empire State Building while standing in the basement." I knew immediately that further, more invasive tests were at hand.

Both the engineer's and the urologist's analogies were of the descriptive variety. Their first obligation was not to persuade but to explain, and that is when analogies are most successful. In medical school, William Harvey was taught in the seventeenth century that blood "ebbs and floods" in the body like tides on a beach. It was an appealing analogy, and for centuries no one questioned it. Then Harvey saw a London fire wagon with two men operating a hand pump, and "Eureka!" he remembered dark venous blood being drawn steadily into the lungs of mammals in his laboratory like water entering the hand pump. He also knew from his experimental work that arterial blood is bright red and under greater pressure. Veins and arteries, he now understood, are "one-way streets," and the heart is a pump midway through the circuit to keep the "traffic" flowing. Amazingly, he knew nothing of the body's "back roads," called capillaries, because the microscopes of his day were not powerful enough to see them. He deduced their existence when all other explanations failed.

In a similar fashion, blind Louis Braille playing dominoes reasoned that people like himself could be taught to read by feeling raised dots pressed into heavy paper like the dots on his toy tiles. Such a description of books for the blind is all well and good, but when analogies form part of an argument, they often mislead and fail. Robert McNamara and other hawkish proponents of American involvement in Viet Nam argued via the infamous Domino Theory: if South Viet Nam falls to the Communists, Cambodia, Laos, Thailand, and others will surely fall in rapid succession. But countries are not tall, unsteady playing tiles. States like Tibet have fallen with little effect on their neighbors. But thanks in part to the misapplication of the domino analogy, perhaps as many as three million people died in Southeast Asia.

Finally, here are two more analogies to test yourself. Is the following proverb descriptive or argumentative: "The whipped dog never betrays its master"?

Because it was used for centuries to justify the physical punishment of English-speaking children, it forms a tight but flawed argument.

Second, a recent description of the *H.L. Hunley*, a Confederate submarine, noted that its hull was heavily encrusted with sand, sediment, and shell. "Removing the crust," said Senior Conservator Paul Mardikian, "will be like removing concrete covering an egg without breaking the shell." Is that sentence descriptive or argumentative?

This explicit and extended comparison attempts to illustrate how delicate and difficult the conservation of the *Hunley* will be. Descriptions may be used in arguments, of course, but Mardikian's succeeds unlike the whipped dog because it is primarily descriptive.

So, if you want fawning children, remember, "The kick of the dam hurts not her colt." As the Chinese say, "Beat your child once a day. If you don't know why, the child knows." If you're still confused, just skip the analogies and follow Elbert Hubbard's advice, "Spare the rod and save the child."

Weeding the Rain Forest: Autobiography

"Gym, tan, laundry—it's the story of my life." —*Anonymous thirty-something*

"The ego rolls best on thirty-five pounds—
neither too hard nor too close to the ground." —*The Wordspinner*

Once was a father who was so disappointed after reading his blue-eyed son's *Who's Who* account that he photocopied, amended, and mailed it to his slighted namesake. Junior, who had no illusions about his fame, measured the single-column entry, then measured his penis and decided he had a Goldilocks sufficiency.

Taking the measure of oneself in print with tongue *in* cheek or *out* is not easy. After Rome fell, it was not just difficult, it was well-nigh impossible for about a thousand years. One notable exception is Augustine's *Confessions in Thirteen Books* (398 AD) which is not so much an autobiography as a lapidary description of how a rough gem came to be polished. Though later canonized, Augustine's chief regret was his inability to recall any more of his sins than he did.

But as the sun rose again on Western Europe about 1350, the Zeitgeist murmured, "Enough about you; it's time for me." Soon Benvenuto Cellini produced an autobiography in which he boasted of killing his enemies while working for the Pope. And soon the relatively flat, unsigned canvasses of Giotto, who left us one disputed self-portrait, deepened into the perspectival works of Albrecht Dürer, who left us at least seven, most signed. Actually they were initialed as if to say, "I don't need to spell it out; you know who I am."

Protestants thought a confessional work like Augustine's flirted with pride, and we all know what pride did for Satan. To this day, many Protestants like the Amish do not keep diaries, have portraits, or use mirrors. Indeed, the faces of Amish dolls are featureless to underscore humanity's equality before God.

The names of Giotto and Dürer, mentioned above, remind us that naming is often a form of biography or even autobiography. Medieval Giotto di Bondone's name means "the immortal one from Bondone, [Italy]." His Renaissance counterpart had two names which mean "the bright, noble door." While these men did not select their own names, many in the late Middle Ages and Renaissance did. One of my favorite illustrations of one who took an autobiographical name is "Philippus Aureolus Theophrastus Bombastus von Hohenheim." Theophrastus, the West's first systematic student of botany, did not bestow this bombastic name on himself, but his "biographers" must have been inordinately proud. Loosely translated, the name means "the golden, horse-loving fellow from Hohenheim, [Switzerland] with hair like fine cotton who speaks with God." After little Theo's ego grew to fit his name, he changed it to "Paracelsus," meaning "equal to" or "better than Celsus," the Roman encyclopedist. "Paracelsus," then, is a truncated autobiography reminiscent of Augustus Caesar, "the *great* Caesar," who was born Octavian, "the eighth child."

History is peppered with people dissatisfied with the names their parents gave them. Mary Ann Evans became "George Eliot" to shield her relationship with a married man. The French "song stylist" Joseph Pujol renamed himself "Le Petomane," ("The Fartiste") because a man shouldn't be ashamed of his art even if it consists of expelling air from his anus into an ocarina. Isabella Baumfree renamed herself "Sojourner Truth" when she became a conductor on the "underground railroad." And Malcolm Little stamped the remains of slavery with an "X" when he could no longer tolerate the slave owner's name he'd inherited.

Whether Catholic or Protestant today, "taking an honest look at oneself" often means snapping a "selfie." Some of the most provocative of these photographs include the lunar astronaut who has the entire Earth reflected in his facemask; the woman, whose day is so scheduled, her face is obliterated by Post-It notes, and the sunken-chested man whose wife's naked breasts behind him hide her husband's ears.

A related genre is the cartoon self-portrait. The continuous-line sketch of Saul Steinberg speaks volumes or a longish paragraph about this Romanian-American cipher. The caricaturist Al Hirschfeld implies the personal nature of his art by removing the top of his head in one drawing and dipping a pen into his brain as he prepares to sign his latest. Best of all is the anonymous drawing in which a female painter touches up a full-length portrait of a confident, besuited man, while "the wizard" himself peeks from behind a curtain.

Just as newspapers are the first draft of history, so are diaries and journals the first drafts of autobiography. The problem with these works is that they soon grow so unwieldy few including this author can bear to read the fading ink in a cantankerous hand. Emerson amassed 182 volumes over fifty-seven years but could never extract the life therein. He did mine them for his essays and poetry, but no life story. At the other extreme is the diarist like my Grandmother Eisiminger who packed seventeen years into one, vest-pocket notebook. From a few telegraphed scratches, I know her car was stolen in 1938 while visiting a hospital, but little more than that.

Whether it's called "I-witness account," "alibi-ography," "autopathography," or "lifelog," the autobiographer may be ashamed to tell her tale "warts and all" and shamed if she doesn't. But the majority, if they ever read it, will read it for the warts, not the all. As I see it, the autobiographer weaves a tapestry, but what's a Gobelin without the knots? Answer: a collection of string too short to save. On the other hand, the life story left for others to relate is ripe for what Rudyard Kipling called the "Higher Cannibalism." Examples include Rufus Griswold's vindictive biography of Poe and Lawrence Thompson's pathographical study of Frost.

❈

Unwilling to hire a "ghost liar" when I retired and not seeing my Boswell near, I decided to sift through the journals I'd kept for forty years with a volume of memoirs in mind. Wanting to leave something fuller than a Wiki stub, mystified by my own blank Facebook page, and knowing that dead men tell no tales, I found myself examining the osmotic membrane between the vibrant life I recalled and the dull life I found in my own handwriting.

Certain I'd been misquoted, and fearing I'd wear out my mirror, I decided to abandon my notes and try something different. I decided to validate a life by writing a series of essays like this one each with a different theme or subject, which I have found interesting and on which I had notes in my card file. At present, I've written 293 essays on subjects ranging from the Absurd to Wordplay. It's true I've added a pinch of spice to some of these for the same reason we stick cloves in a ham.

Another journal project, which Joan Didion rightly observes helps us "keep on nodding terms with the people we used to be," entails collecting cartoons which relate to my life and the family's. Perversely determined to see myself as a comic figure, I have annotated these strips and panels for the grandchildren and pasted these in a notebook. The oyster has its pearl to muse; I have what may resemble a mockumentary, but it's really a love letter.

It's a Book—It Has No Joystick: Books and Libraries

"I am a proud non-reader of books." —*Kanye West*

"In Bunraku…, the chief reader holds out the text and bows to it…." —*Susan Sontag*

I do not own a Kindle, Nook, or iPad, and I have no intention of purchasing one either. That is unless the makers enable a user to highlight a passage and copy it the way I print from an email or web document. Until that happens, I'll continue to invest in print media. As I have said elsewhere, if heaven has no books, magazines, or newspapers, preferably in hard copies, I do not want to go there. I simply owe paper, ink and traditional libraries too much to give up on them now. I know the Sumerians thought clay tablets would be the recording medium for eternity just as the Egyptians believed in papyrus, and medieval Europeans bought stock in Pergamese parchment. But until Kindle's pixels can be conveniently transferred to a sheet of foolscap, I'll put my faith in paper.

At seventy-four, I now have shelves of vinyl and tape recordings that I can no longer listen to. I can imagine discarded piles of e-books at mid-century when some all-too foreseeable technology enables every book and musical composition to be implanted in one's brain. If or when that happens, whoever inherits my paper files (estimated weight 1000 pounds) will enjoy peace of mind knowing that they are going nowhere. If an item becomes too fragile, it can always be photocopied and returned to the file for another generation to read and fondle.

Just as Holden Caulfield positioned himself at the base

of a cliff to rescue the children tumbling over the precipice, I have been a catcher of books. I'm not a collector, however; I'm a reader—I catch and release. Readers are those who might peruse *The Great Gatsby* a dozen times over twenty years and copy something fresh from each excursion in their card file or commonplace book. A collector, on the other hand, is one who sneers at the paperback *Gatsbys* in Books-a-Million, yet spends $5,000 on a first edition with a pristine dust jacket. He'll then shrink-wrap the poor thing and place it in a safety-deposit box. The value of a book, however, lies not in what it does for our balance sheet but what it does to prod our minds and touch our hearts.

As for catching and releasing books, once I've finished, I place them in a pile outside my office for anyone who wants them. After my friends and students had picked through the latest pile, I gave the remainder to the Clemson library. The librarians kept a few and sold the rest, but none went to the dump. I recall finding a dumpster half-full of books in front of the Columbus (Georgia) Public Library. Not one that I could reach turned to dust when I opened it, so I asked the head librarian if he couldn't stack the books in the lobby and place a "Free Books to a Good Home" sign overhead. He said he didn't like it any more than I did, but state law forbade giving away or selling books bought with public funds. The Jews, I've read, solemnly bury a book that has outlived its usefulness, but I've yet to see one that couldn't be read at least one more time regardless of whose money bought it.

Despite one woman's instructions in her will to bind her lover's novels in her skin, no book deserves a human sacrifice. Hitler's *Mein Kampf* proves that point, but neither would I burn all remaining copies of it either. The books that come closest to iconic status in the West include Shakespeare's First Folio, Copernicus's *On the Revolutions of Heavenly Spheres*, Gutenberg's Bible, and Audubon's *Birds of America*. Every known copy of these four including the marginalia has been lovingly catalogued. Yet for all our reverence, only Audubon's has not been on someone's *Index Expurgatorius* at one time or another. Indeed, books have been targeted so often that one Oxford college kept its volumes tethered with chains until 1799. Indeed, Hereford Cathedral still has its collection chained to the shelves, but this is mainly for the tourists.

Students from abroad are often amazed at the American open-stack system and public library accommodations. Think bookmobile. Indeed, in 1986, the Chicago Public Library System had about 7,500 copies of *The Catcher in the Rye* that were so long overdue they were listed as lost, yet the system continued to buy Salinger's novel. Perhaps no library has bent so far backwards as Vienna's City Library: until 2006, the librarians at that hoary but tolerant institution would read "literary erotica" on the telephone to patrons for a nominal charge.

I began by admitting my anti-technology bias, but I'll close with admiration for those who are working to put every book written on-line for free. Google has not asked permission to place my corpus in the public domain, but they are welcome to it. Personally, I'd rather have someone read a book of mine than collect a royalty, but then I don't make my living entirely with a pen.

Despite some Luddite tendencies, I never cease to be amazed at what technology is doing for researchers and readers: I read recently that 95% of *all* humanistic and scientific inquiries begin with Google. In 2009, I was looking for a book that the Clemson Library did not own, so I went to the interlibrary loan office on the fourth floor where the librarian turned to his computer, typed in worldcat.org, and in seconds, I knew that the Anderson Public Library about fifteen miles away and the Furman Library about thirty miles away had a copy of the out-of-print title. Now I could have driven to either location in under an hour, but I was not pressed for time, so I asked for the book to be delivered. Two days later, it was in my office mail box. By contrast, some Irish librarians in the eighteenth century locked their patrons in carrels to prevent precious books from wandering.

While I was marveling over WorldCat, the ILL librarian said that as recently as 1995 Oxford students had to wait an average of two hours while a book just a few meters away passed through thirteen hands before the patron could open it. I said that open stacks are a blessing but wished more students appreciated them. Indeed, a friend of mine who works in the university bookstore has noticed a disturbing phenomenon: scholarship athletes who pay nothing for their textbooks often sell them back to the bookstore a semester later still in their cellophane wrappers.

Alan Fletcher observed that books resemble humans in that many have a preface, body, spine, back, appendix, and footnotes. We reach maturity when we recognize that taken as a whole these "people" are more trustworthy reporting the Truth than our parents regardless of how much they love us. And though technophiles today sneer at "treeware," my heart is still in the tenth century with Abdul Kassem Ismael, the Grand Vizier of Persia. Ismail took his 117,000 volume library strapped to four hundred camels wherever he traveled. To expedite his reading pleasure, his "bookmobile" had been trained to walk in alphabetical order. You'll have to trust me on this, but if he'd been able to transport his library in a Kindle, the inns and oases where he spent the night would not have been the same.

Stray Hyphens in a Dirty-Movie House: Clarity

"During Lentil season, I give up sweets
or celibate sex and other sweetmeats." —*The Wordspinner*

"I toast the candor of one who betook,
in his 'Errata' to put 'the whole book.'" —*The Wordspinner*

During the Cold War, about the time I was completing my enlistment in the Army Security Agency, the Army's branch of the NSA, I saw a poster in the company dayroom lavished with palm trees and sandy beaches asking, "Are you ready to see Southeast Asia?" For all the warmth it offered, I was not.

In 2009, I heard a radio ad posted by the CIA asking, "Are you ready for a world of ambiguity and adventure?" Answer: still no, for I'd had my fill of fog. From late-1960 to mid-1963, my brothers in arms and I had sat on Bahrdorf's "Gallows Hill" within sight of the East German border gathering any stray electronic pulse or amplified syllable from the East that we could capture on audio tape. But what it all meant, "the big picture," the soldiers at the grasping end of the intelligence octopus never knew. Ignorance was no doubt a good thing in the event that we were captured, but faced with the ethical ambiguity of continuing to read our neighbor's mail, as a writer and human being, I was ready to abandon obfuscation and embrace clarity.

Since then, as a "word-spinning" versifier (see the epigraphs above), I sometimes fail in my resolve to communicate clearly, but I excuse that failure in the name of "richness," the two-for-the-price-of-one deal I offer my readers. "Poems dance," as Diane Ackerman puts it, "with many veils," and as they fall, the reader's insight deepens.

As a teacher of expository prose, however, I was frustrated when any editor returned something of mine with a question mark in the margin. One such return was so egregious that I saved it to remind myself of the instructive embarrassment. Browsing in the Clemson library's Special Collections, I found some unpublished letters written to and by Abe Davidson, a local sculptor, and I thought I might make a short essay out of them. Though an immigrant, Davidson was Clemson's own, and he is cherished for, among other works, the seated concrete statue of the school's founder, Thomas Green Clemson, or "Old Green Tom" as the students dubbed him when he was later recast in bronze. "As a boy in Russia," as I wrote in a draft for the *Clemson World*, "Davidson carved buxom women into wooden canes for soldiers after WWI, for there were many then who need help walking." My editor wrote back, "He carved *what*?" The ambiguity was, of course, some textual and tactile "richness" I had not intended, so I replied saying I could comprehend what I'd written, but I could not explain it.

Encounters such as this one helped to make me tolerant of my students' miscues. Before the first quiz in an interdisciplinary humanities class, I had discussed several topics including mosaic art and a few books in the Old Testament, reputedly by Moses. On the quiz, one question asked for a brief description of ancient "mosaic art," and a solid-C student answered by discussing the artistry of Job, or what he took to be "Mosaic art." As the student pointed out, in any oral discussion of "mosaic art," there is no way to know if "mosaic" is capitalized or not. I docked him three points and gave him two, for our text had numerous examples of Greek mosaics as well as references to Moses.

Student writing is littered with references to "morpheme tablets," "unauthorized autobiographies," "World War Too," and "Tiresias, the blind profit." But I tip my hat to the A. P. Government student who realized that medical science made the U. S. Constitution ambiguous about a century after it was ratified. The clever student realized that the phrase "natural-born citizen" could conceivably disqualify some candidate who was born via cesarean. The phrase in question was inserted by the framers to protect us from "foreign influences," but they never dreamed of a year when 30% of American births are accomplished by C-section. Indeed, many medical and scientific advances seem to obnubilate the doctrines and dogmas of the past just as "obnubilate" clouds this sentence.

From backing up a trailer, to flesh-eating plants, to quantum mechanics, the physical world often seems counter-intuitive, but most of us adjust even if we don't understand. Of course, humans are under no more obligation to understand the world than it's obligated to make sense. The sun, a paradox in itself, lightens hair but darkens the skin. The elements sodium and chlorine are fatal if ingested, but compounded as sodium chloride, a "pinch" is necessary for the body's proper functioning, while a "pound" is fatal. Unreasonable as salt's behavior is, I'm inclined to give the "paradoxical frog" top honors, for its tadpole is three times larger than the adult. I imagine the amphibian father croaking with pride and the mother in shock, given that the disparity cannot be reasoned by human or beast from the context.

In 1934, Gertrude Stein was asked by an NBC radio reporter to explain a passage in her libretto, *Four Saints in Three Acts*: "Pigeons on the grass alas. Pigeons on the grass alas. Short longer grass short longer longer shorter yellow grass." Stein replied that the explanation was "simple." At the end of one summer, she'd been walking in a public park, as she explained, when she saw some birds in the dying grass, so she sat down and wrote until she had emptied herself of the emotion. The reporter wondered, "How is the reader supposed to know what you are thinking about?" And Stein replied, "The reader knows because he enjoys it." But I wonder. Were Stein's emotions or are the readers' so simple, and are they entirely enjoyable? When I read her lines above, I wondered as Ron Moran, a poet-friend of mine, has written, "Are pigeons on the roof, aloof?"

Indeed, ambiguity is seldom as simple as deciding whether to buy "a vacuum cleaner that sucks," and often, it's fatal. I'm thinking of the tragic "charge of the light brigade" in the Crimean War. In short, one British officer told another to charge some exposed Russian artillerymen. The second officer, who surely did not understand the original command, ordered his men with a gallant wave of his arm to mount their horses and charge a well-entrenched position instead. The result was 270 needless deaths. As Robert Graves later wrote, "Even in the calmest times, it is ... difficult to compose an English sentence that cannot possibly be misunderstood." But what choice do we have except to try?

✳

One busy day in the Jupiter offices of the Florida Inland Navigational District, a Fed Ex driver entered and asked my father if he'd sign for the envelope the driver had under his arm. Dad agreed, signed the form, and tossed the envelope on his absent secretary's littered desk. A few hours later, he saw the envelope again and tore it open.

Inside was a cashier's check for 2.2 million dollars with the unmistakable words, "pay to the bearer." He then checked the address on the envelope and understood the driver's mistake: Dad's office was at 1314 Marcinski Road, not 3959 Marcinski where a BB&T branch was located two blocks away. The idea of cashing it and leaving town crossed his mind, but he wisely decided to call the bank's manager. As he later told me, "$2.2 million would have made a tidy nest egg, but my finances are adequate. At my age [81], I don't need any more fog." Clarity was his ethic and part of his legacy to his children.

Rein and Spur: Classic vs. Romantic

"The road to excess leads to the palace of wisdom."
—*William Blake*

"Neither excess nor abstinence has made man any happier."
—*Voltaire*

Shortly after my wife and I moved into the house we still occupy thirty-five years later, she planted a bed of pansies beside the brick patio I had just laid out on a bed of sand. Call it obsessiveness or pride of ownership, but I surveyed my patio almost daily for spindly green aliens rising between my red bricks. A year or so later after a week's vacation, we returned to find "weeds" coming up next to the flower bed. I dropped the suitcases and started uprooting these upstarts.

"Wait!" Ingrid cried, "Those are pansies!"

"If they grow between the bricks, they're weeds." After a brief "discussion," reason yielded to the romantic appreciation of nonconformist nature. When the bags were unpacked, I pried the bricks out of the sand, and transplanted the pansies to the flower bed. While she was cooking supper, I sprayed an herbicide on my bricks, and order was restored.

In time, I captured the moment in a crotchet called "Aesthetic Quandary":

A volunteer pansy
grows from a brick.
Romantics say, "Leave her."
Classics say, "Pick."

A year or so later, I decided to extend my bricks around

the house in the form of a path. I preferred a simple rectangular pattern that followed the house's outline while Ingrid desired something that "meandered." "Meander," of course, won the day, and I retired to write "Romantic Wife Chastens Her Husband":

Ere you pave a straight path
down to the tarn,
meander the route
the cows take to the barn.

Were I more of a romantic like Sir Walter Scott, I would have shot a bird, plucked and split a primary feather, dipped my quill in its blood, and inscribed my verses on the cuff of my silk sleeve. John Muir, another romantic at heart, often wrote using sequoia sap. As for myself and the two poems you've just read, I retired to my study when I found time to write, searched for Edgar Poe's "tarn," scanned the *Penguin Rhyming Dictionary*, and settled back to write on my Dell PC. Neither blood nor sap is an option on my printer.

But believe it or not, I wasn't cloned from Alexander Pope. When I was about fourteen, I used to race up the hill behind our house to climb the tallest pine every time I heard thunder. There I'd sit swaying in the wind, soaked to the skin, shaking my fist at Thor. I rather doubt the "wasp of Twickenham" ever climbed a tree even on a clear day. "Nature" to that archetypal classicist usually meant "human nature." He viewed the world so broadly that his idea of a speckled trout was one of "the scaly breed" or "finny tribe." Though Pope was not a painter, he resembled his French contemporary Francois Boucher who complained that "nature is too green and badly lit." The arch-romantic Ludwig van Beethoven, on the other hand, said he loved trees more than humans. Deafness has been known to do that to people.

Like Karl Shapiro, I prefer to think of what my son and I did rescuing the half-acre lot my wife and I live on as "carving the wilderness into decorum." Shapiro was referring to Thomas Jefferson's building of Monticello, and our modest home is hardly that, but it was built in what had been a wilderness of honeysuckle vines and green thorn. Despite the meandering brick path that rings the house, it does possess a decorous air.

Aware that I might have lost some of you who have been busy "getting and spending" or just hunting for gainful employment the last few years, let me make the classic-romantic distinction a bit sharper and less personal.

- Are you a fence or open-pasture person?
- Does the draftsman's line appeal to you or the intensity of Monet's palette?
- Does satire tickle your brain, or does a lyric move you to tears?
- Is sex better in the bedroom on or in a forest lit by fireflies?
- Do you prefer the architecture of the US Capitol or the Smithsonian's "castle?"
- Do you like your arches round or pointed?
- Would you rather take a golf cart through the gardens of Williamsburg or hike through Yellowstone?
- Is caffeine your stimulant of choice or absinthe?
- Does Caesar Augustus arouse your imagination or Dracula?
- Are you a deist or pantheist—did your God create the universe and die in the Big Bang, or is She still present in every rock and leaf?
- Is Ben Franklin's Armonica your instrument of choice or the Aeolian harp—thirty-seven glass bowls on

a horizontal axle or a box full of tuned strings sitting in an open window?

• Would you turn to a school-marmish dictionary like Samuel Johnson's or the no-holds-barred Oxford English Dictionary?

• Is education a "filling up" or a "leading out"?

• Would you rather dance a minuet or waltz?

• Does your writing target a worldwide audience or is it written chiefly to please yourself?

• Are you partial to the US Constitution with its balance of powers or the Bill of Rights which may or may not allow you to carry a gun in public?

• Are you drawn more to Apollo or Dionysus?

• Does your "*Cogito*" begin "I think" or "I feel"?

• And finally, do you think an artist's best work comes after a lifetime of seasoning, or is she washed up, as Goethe thought, at twenty-eight?

If most of your preferences are from the first half of the above pairs, your tastes are decidedly classical, and vice versa.

Too many questions, you say. Then consider this comic chestnut: the Persian romantic poet Omar Khayyam wrote that all he needed was "a loaf of bread, a jug of wine, and thou." How he planned to pay his rent is unstated. The classically minded critic reads Omar's line, and at some point notes that the three have a common denominator: each may produce a yeast infection. See the difference now?

If not, I have one more trick up my sleeve drawn from the history of architecture. About 1780 as the Neo-Classical era was peaking in Europe, Francois Racine de Monville, despite the stirrings of revolt in France, completed what many consider the ultimate tribute to classical antiquity: a home inside a fifty-foot-tall fluted column. Call it the folly of a classically trained man who understood the limitations of reason. Monsieur de Monville had a romantic side as well, for he built his four-stories connected by a helical staircase inside a "ruin." The ragged top of his home looks (for it still stands) as if Zeus had snapped off the upper half of the column and devoured the capital. Like Marie Antoinette, who was a guest here once, de Monville reportedly hired a hermit to stroll about the grounds to lend them *gravitas*. Nothing is more romantic than an ornamental hermit.

More like white and black than good and evil, there's no right or wrong in the classic-romantic dualism. The two sides represent either end of the arc of a pendulum swung by the tastes of the dominant class. It has swung for centuries, and though unpredictable, it shows no signs of slowing. One moment my wits clamber for attention, the next it's my heart. Last Sunday I went for a barefoot jog only to come home and pull weeds from between my bricks.

From Tribal Drums to Deaf Babies: Communication

"Spoken words are often the tiniest darts—
unfelt rays that pass through the heart." —*The Wordspinner*

"I once thought action spoke louder than words,
not knowing soft-spoken is more often heard." —*The Wordspinner*

If the earliest advocates of clear discourse lived "BC," I am "BT," "Before Twitter." Nevertheless, I can fire off an email at light speed and begrudge those who check their mail but once a day. I once earned a merit badge in part by flashing a mirror in the sun, but I do not tweet. I can send you an SOS in Morse code, but you cannot page me. I telephone, snail mail, voice mail, Facebook, and text, but I do not Instagram. However, given that my first text was sent less than a year ago, I may yet be swept up by the "smart mob."

I may have inherited my communication skills from my father. I don't think they originated any earlier because "sittin' and rockin'" was my grandfathers' idea of communicating with the grandchildren. However, in 1927, Dad built a crystal radio set which he placed on the floor of the living room, the family "museum." He covered his device with a large metal bowl from his mother's kitchen, so he and up to three of his four siblings could press an ear to the bowl and listen to the Cardinals' games broadcast from across the river. Suddenly the museum had a new exhibit, and it was live.

Crossing the Rhine in 1945, Dad's self-taught skills may have saved his life and the lives of his men. Fortunately, he'd memorized the radio frequency the British were operating on that night, so when the "friendly" guns on the west bank lit up, he placed an urgent call to the battery commander and the firing ceased.

In 1959, Dad called his Northern Virginia home from a radio telephone while flying over Turkey in a military plane. I thought that 5,000 mile transoceanic call was the squirrel's pearl until President Nixon, sitting in the Oval Office, conversed with two astronauts, standing on the moon.

Yet for all his communication skills, Dad fit the prototype defined by Hans Jurgens: after eight years of marriage, the average Western couple reaches a state of "almost total speechlessness." I should have suspected my parents' stalemate, for when I telephoned home and Dad answered, he'd often say, "Hi, Skip—let me get your mother." The truth dawned when Mother lay in bed following a stroke, and I flew to Arizona for eleven days to see her for the last time. Once as Dad and I were approaching her hospital room, he said, "You speak to her today; you know what to say." I was shocked that after sixty years of marriage any husband didn't know what to say.

Knowing the burden was on me, I began reading the morning paper with an eye toward sharing it with Mother. I clipped short articles and comic strips that I thought she'd find interesting or induce a smile. Often a cartoon would lead to, "Do you remember the time Dad did the same thing?" Dad would then deny it; Mother would make a slight correction, but our laughter was all the evidence I needed to continue.

Erich Fromm argued that the essence of love is gift giving, but he wasn't referring to blue boxes tied with a ribbon from Tiffany's. The gifts are, as Fromm wrote, a mix of one's joy, interest, understanding, knowledge, humor, sadness, indeed, "all manifestations of that which is alive in oneself." Since reading *The Art of Loving*, I try never to dine without something to share with my partner or partners. If anyone cares enough to cook us a meal, I think it's incumbent on me to return the favor. Recently when my wife passed me a plate of sliced tomatoes, I said, "I'll take the heels; you know how much I love them." For the two of us, this naturally segued into a conversation contrasting my wife's mother, who was serious when she uttered that memorable sentence, and those like myself who prefer a thick, center cut. It was a small gesture on my part, but anything which sustains the memory of our sainted Mom is a gift unmatched in Tiffany's catalogue.

※

Though bottled water killed water-cooler gossip, and email has killed many an office coffee lounge, there's never been a time when humans are more connected. We seem to have recognized that interpersonal communication is fundamental to our welfare and that technology is finally accommodating this need. But before petroglyphs became pixelgrams, we'd had excellent communication skills for at least 50,000 years and perhaps a million. We didn't always use them, but often we did. When in the sixteenth century Michelangelo's servant could not read his master's shopping list, the artist sketched pictures of the herring and tortelli he wanted. When in the nineteenth century Lewis needed Clark, he set the prairie on fire. Lock a man in solitary in any century, and he'll find some way to tap out code. Deaf babies will babble with their hands, and when deaf mothers cannot read the lips of their children in ski masks, they read their semaphoring brows. And when a colleague's shy student could not bring himself to speak in class, he found relief speaking through a sock puppet.

Henry Thoreau feared that after the Maine-to-Texas telegraph line was completed, Maine and Texas might discover they have "nothing important to communicate." That would have been a failure of mind, however, not technology. Likewise, a Los Angeles Police Department review in 1994 revealed that "bad communication" ranked first among the causes for "errors in shooting" by its officers. If there was ever a time that the police carried knives or clubs instead of handguns, there surely were fewer accidental killings. Still, it wasn't the technology that failed in 1994, it was the officers' failure to communicate.

My favorite image of communication failure, however, is the young couple I once saw strolling their twins on College Avenue in Clemson. The adults were using their tablets; the kids were using Baby Einstein, but no one spoke or showed any emotion. For the few minutes I followed them, I fought the urge to yank out their ear buds to end what technology consultant Linda Stone has called their "continuous partial attention." I realize this couple may have been practicing "mindfulness," but the example they set for their twins was smugly asocial as they breezed past pedestrians smiling at or speaking to their twins.

But surely the successes of modern communication are more notable than the failures of the "self-phone." In the fifteenth century, Leonardo da Vinci foresaw a day when "men shall speak to one another...though they stand in different hemispheres and...shall understand each other." The home computer, cellphone, and spread of English (to places like China, where more people speak English in 2015 than in the US and UK combined) prove the accuracy of the prediction.

※

Three closing parables must suffice to illustrate bad, good, and sublime communications.

First, the bad: following a training exercise in the south of Germany, Lt. Gilstrap informed the drivers of fifteen vehicles that he had "a hot date four hundred miles to the north," and he didn't want any whining about stopping for something to eat or a place to urinate. Off the convoy went, up the Autobahn until an MP stopped our lieutenant for speeding and issued him a citation for each vehicle. His date and military career on hold, the lieutenant demanded to know why the vehicles at the back of the convoy had not radioed him to slow down. The ranking NCO bravely reminded the lieutenant that he'd ordered information to flow down the chain of command, not up.

Next, the good: when a single mother and her overactive son found themselves at odds following a frightful divorce, the mother sought help. In due time, her therapist led them to a rock-climbing wall in a gymnasium on the same block. There the therapist blindfolded the thirteen-year-old and instructed his mother to tell her son where to place his hands and feet so that he might scale the wall he could not see. After a few visits to the gym, trust was restored and the flow of words between them improved.

Finally, the sublime: in Jan van Eyck's *Annunciation*, the artist recorded the dialogue between Gabriel and Mary in the oils he pioneered. As guest, Gabriel sweetly greets his hostess, "Hail, [Mary] full of grace," three words in Latin streaming in diaphanous gold across the canvas. Mary replies, "Behold, [I am] the handmaiden of the Lord." Her words of acknowledgement and submission, however, are written upside down and backwards for the convenience of her Father, the father of her child.

Nano Lit: Concision

"In laboring to be brief, I become obscure." —*Horace*

"[Concision] is almost a condition of being inspired." —*George Santayana*

Though Teddy Roosevelt's life was spared when an assassin's bullet was slowed by the fifty-page speech tucked in his vest pocket, five hundred words saw Moses through the creation. As a writer, I harken to the Mosaic example, and in this, I am assisted by my mother tongue: English by every test that I have applied is the most economical of the world's major languages. Thumb through the Hexaglot Bible next time you're in the library, and of the six languages represented there, the English column is invariably the shortest.

My respect for linguistic economy, however, originated with Professor Ruth Faulk's bleeding pen. It was she who swore like Attila that "every slaughtered syllable is a good deed." Once she ordered a thousand-word essay and returned it a few days later with instructions to write it again in five hundred. Channeling Emily Dickinson and Ernest Hemingway, she convinced me that the best writing is a hardwood, striped of its bark, sawn, planed, and dried in the sun.

Another mentor of mine, Professor James Dickey, urged his "nest of singing birds" to write reams of heroic couplets "ere venturing anything longer." I was pleased that he liked my curtal couplet: "Round Robin Hood's barn / makes a tedious yarn." Not just brief, he said, but concise.

After flying from Dickey's nest, and inspired by the flash-fiction revival of the 1990s, I started collecting examples of what I broadly call "nano lit": prodigies of written or spoken concision. Here's an example of each flash genre I've contrived:

- Flash oratory: "The Gettysburg Address," At 272 words, Abraham Lincoln's speech is still the best a human has spoken in English. The orator who preceded Lincoln spoke for two hours, and no one today recalls a word of what he said.
- Flash non-fiction: "$E=MC^2$," Albert Einstein
- Flash war communiqué: "Sighted sub, sank same." Donald F. Mason
- Flash telegram: "Stop." Anon.
- Flash film review: "I'm a Camera": "No Leica." Goodman Ace
- Flash poem: Edmund Conti's "Potholes": *A void*.
- Flash suicide note: "My work is done. Why wait?" George Eastman
- Flash koan: "Wherever you go, there you are." Anon.
- Flash Oscar speech: "Thank you." Wm. Holden
- Flash sermon: "Be kind." Anon.
- Flash recipe: "Moose stew: Shoot one moose." Anon.
- Flash tweet: "tl; dr." ["Too long; didn't read."] Anon.
- Flash paraphrase: New Testament: "He was born. He lived. He died. He's coming back. He's not going to be happy." Anon.
- Flash monologue: "'Shut up,' [Daddy] explained." Ring Lardner
- Flash professional fiction: "For sale: baby shoes, never worn." Ernest Hemingway
- Flash ballet instructions: "1. Don't fall. 2. Get up."

Alexander Pushkin

• Flash homework: Write a short story with these elements: religion, royalty, sex, mystery. Sample "A+" story: "My God," said the queen. "I'm pregnant. I wonder who did it." Anon.

• Flash corporate slogan: "Think." IBM

• Flash SAT Essay: "You ask if tradition and progress ever conflict. Yes, tradition and progress sometimes conflict." Anon. Despite its admirable brevity, it was graded "F."

• Flash crime novel: "Bang!" Anon.

• Flash admonition: "You can't have everything. Where would you put it?" Steven Wright

• Flash resignation: "Dear Sir: I quit." Anon.

• Flash marriage acceptance speech: "You had me at 'Hello.'" Renée Zellweger in *Jerry Maguire*

• Flash ad: "For sale, parachute, used once." Anon.

• Flash bench judgment: Replying to a delinquent taxpayer who said, "As God is my judge, I do not owe this tax," Judge Howard Dawson said, "He isn't. I am. You do."

• Flash cinema: "Fred Ott's Sneeze." Filmed in 1894 by William K. L. Dickson, it lasts five seconds.

• Flash conclusion: "Etc." Anon.

• Flash architectural dogma: "Less is more." Mies van der Rohe

• Flash rebuttal: "Less is a bore." Robert Venturi

• Flash will: "All to wife." Karl Tausch scrawled this on the wall beside his death bed. Compare this will to Frederica E. S. Cook's which ran 1066 pages bound in four volumes.

• Flash obit: "De Sade, Donatien Alphonse. French soldier, pervert." Anon.

- Flash last words: "They couldn't hit an elephant at this distance." Gen. John Sedgwick
- Flash epitaph: "I should have been cremated." Anon.

※

Albert Einstein once urged an audience to make everything as simple as possible but not simpler. I learned the wisdom of that observation when I, as head of the English humanities section, emailed my department head, "Would there be any objection if [name of an untenured lecturer deleted] teaches a 300-level humanities class next semester?"

The head replied, "No way!"

I replied, "No way that you have an objection, or no way that she'll teach a 300-level course?"

He replied, "No objection."

Clearly, the department head had oversimplified this issue to the point of obfuscation and nearly to the point of libel.

Not long after this exchange, a student brought a "D" paper to my office asking how he could raise his grade. Without rereading it, I took one look at his emaciated paragraphs and suggested a robust regime for the development of his ideas.

"So, you want me to wordy it up, professor?"

"No, of course not," I said and explained that while his "riprap rocks" *was* "wordied up," I was aiming for something more refined. I then told him how Ezra Pound had reduced his poem of thirty lines to two and in doing so had given birth to Imagism. I told him I didn't expect anything that grand and showed him how a colleague had cut five pages from the university's faculty manual by substituting

"Provost" for "Provost and Vice President for Academic Affairs."

✳

I'll close with a flash anecdote which attempts to negotiate the fine line between too much information and too little. It's closer to what I was hoping my students would produce in the narrative assignment I'd given them.

"Heirs to the Mt. Olive pickle fortune, Dean Morris Cox and his wife, Irene, lived many years on a boggy acre with a stream meandering through their front yard. Both were long-time wildflower enthusiasts living as they were on the banks of a small Lake Hartwell tributary. So when Lake Jocassee in the mountains to the north began rising toward 'full pond,' and a friend whose property was scheduled to be inundated invited the dean to transplant a few Oconee Bells, Morris leapt at the opportunity to assist an endangered species.

After several hours of digging and hauling the plants to the trunk of his Rolls-Royce, he headed home in muddy clothes and boots. On the way back to Clemson, he stopped in a country grocery to buy a soft drink and a pack of peanuts. As he waited to pay, the customer in front of him dropped a dime. Always the gentleman, Morris picked it up and offered it to its rightful owner. After giving his deanship a quick assessment, the customer said, 'Keep it— you look like you need it more than I do.'

So Morris quietly pocketed the coin, paid for his purchases, and went back to his Rolls. As he was preparing to leave, the careless customer tapped on the driver's-side window. While Morris was still rolling it down, the man stuck his nose inside and said, 'I want my dime back.'"

Wet Flags Wrapped at Half-Mast: General and Specific

Writers should not substitute "scrupulous enumeration" for "the grandeur of generality...." —*Samuel Johnson*

"Give local habitation to airy nothing." —*Emily Dickinson*

While posting final grades in December of 1986, a colleague in microbiology was rudely confronted by one of his students. The sophomore pre-med major introduced himself and demanded to know why he'd failed one of his prerequisites. The aging professor, who had no recollection of the young man, worried he might have made a mistake. He, therefore, pulled out his grade book, located the student, and made a few mental calculations. "Well," he said finally, "there's no mistake. In the simplest terms, you failed because your final average was 57, or three points below passing."

"But what's three lousy points?" asked the student.

After another considered pause, the colleague said, "Well, let's put it this way: what were three degrees of temperature on that cold morning the Challenger lifted off? Or, to bring my analogy closer to Earth, what are three scratches on the new BMW you're about to take possession of? Or, teleologically speaking, what are three sins if God permits none?"

"Hell!" said the student.

"Exactly," said the professor.

The semester before my colleague made his point so concretely about the necessity of standards, I was teaching a Structure of Poetry class. With the space shuttle's twisted "Y" in the sky still fresh in most minds, I decided to teach the heroic couplet with a new twist. Each of the three two-line verses the students were assigned to produce had to allude to the tragedy via Eliot's objective correlative. In other words, I wanted my young writers to deal with verities like courage, honor, and grief, but I wanted them to express themselves in concrete imagery. It's been about thirty years, but one submission titled "In the Wake" is still lodged in my brain:

"Heavy in the darkness, limp at half-mast,
the post office flag is silence aghast."

I'd tell you who performed this small miracle, but the neurons that once coded the author's name have long since died. Concrete imagery, however, does not dissolve so readily. And that relative stability is why I advise younger writers to observe a rough 70-30 split between the concrete and the abstract. The physician who listens to your heart and says, "It could be anything" needs to buy something specific at the general store. On the other hand, the chemist who tells his girlfriend her hair has the fragrance of sodium sulfonate should visit the same store and buy something general. Success lies in the proportions.

Perhaps my preference for the Keatsian particular stems from reading *A Farewell to Arms* as a young man just a few kilometers from the East German-Russian war machine while the Berlin Wall was being built. As Hemingway observed, "Abstract words such as *glory, honor, courage*, or *hallow* were obscene beside the concrete names of villages, the numbers of roads, the names of rivers, the numbers of regiments, and the dates." Though Keats recommended loading "every rift with ore," I think 70% is a better target in prose.

Browsing in Hume or Kant, I find myself longing for a nightingale or a Grecian urn. Reading philosophy for this student of the humanities is like reading song titles off a record spinning at 45 rpm. After returning to the start of one of Kant's sentences for the nth time, I wrote in the margin, "Caution: whiplash!" To illustrate the difficulties presented by language devoid of the sand and gravel that concrete requires, I decided to retell the story of Jesus' birth using Christmas carols as a springboard. Here's how it starts: "A thing befell at twenty-four hours Zulu; the visibility was good. While ovine herders chaperoned their woolly charges, one could hear the seraphic harbingers vocalize. Though cherubim were aurally located in the ozone, it was, nevertheless, a taciturn eventide. Lo, small Palestinian village south of Jerusalem, how is it that you were gleaned from the chaff of small municipalities? Regardless, it was a pious crepuscule that brought our monarchs triune to their prayer bones by a distant, bovine feed box...."

I close this farce advising, "Gussy up the galleries, tintinabulate the tintinabula, and call up the wee, male timpanist, for Kris Kringle is converging on the metropolis!"

All of which is not to say that abstraction does not have its place in the artist's toolbox. The subtle chromatic shifts of the Rothko Chapel in Houston, the slashing, black-on-white canvases of Franz Kline, the elephant ballets of Alexander Calder's mobiles, and Mozart's absolute symphonies are all successful because each work is ecumenically transparent.

Indeed, without a leavening of the abstract, the concrete may fail. Here's an example of a "concrete poem" that disappoints on several levels:

oceanoceanocean
oceancanoeocean
oceanoceanocean

As critics used to say of Salvator Dali, the cleverness of

this poem does not extend above its wrist. Yes, "canoe" is an anagram for "ocean," but would anyone paddle such a craft into the Pacific hunting whale? God lives in the detail but so does the devil. Perhaps the poet should have written:

   tidetidetide
  tidekayaktide
  tidetidetide

The palindromic kayak has been the Inuits' preferred mode of transport for centuries because no one does an "Eskimo roll" in a canoe even if it is covered. But either way, that inch-long canoe in the first poem looks helpless in its shoebox of waves, and perhaps that is what the anonymous poet was reaching for: a visual image of helplessness: Pi on a raft with a tiger in the lifeboat. Still, readers have a right to expect more from poets than a simple appeal to the eye.

✳

Coach John Wooden, whose basketball teams at UCLA won ten national championships in twelve years, used to begin his freshman camp by demonstrating how to put on socks. This detail may have seemed peripheral to his players, but as Wooden often said, "Little things make big things happen." That very general observation, however, is meaningless unless the coach has a pair of clean socks and two naked feet to dress. Indeed, his players succeeded in part because seldom did any of them have to sit out a game with a blister.

Mind Play: Conversation

"Silence is a sketchpad on which we draw,
assuming a line is drawn from our craw." —*The Wordspinner*

"Our talk in the parlor is dry and small—
thoughtful speech blossoms when tossing a ball."—*The Wordspinner*

To encourage civility and stimulate conversation, Catherine II posted several rules for her Russian and foreign guests. Excluded from the Hermitage after 1770 were all hats, swords, insignia and yawns. Moreover, she urged her visitors to refrain from "gnaw[ing] on anything."

Inexperienced as I am with public "gnawing," I imagine there must have been a good reason to ban it from polite company, for it does appear to discourage social intercourse of all kinds. But what *does* stimulate pleasant discourse has not changed fundamentally since Catherine's day. Imagine the table talk of Einstein and Freud over cigars and Drambuies. Though Einstein understood psychology about as well as Freud understood physics, both were sincerely curious about the other's field; thus, Freud said, the interplay was delightful.

Another conversational stimulant is the seating arrangement: do the seats face each other or a viewing screen? If the furniture is arranged in a "C," or "V," I head for the kitchen. Here is where the women usually congregate, and it's here that one generally finds better conversations than in most macho lairs.

I recall one Thanksgiving when I stumbled into the basement and found two male relatives in a tryptophanic stupor "watching" a football game. In truth, the teams were so mismatched, I could not blame them. Several hours before my customary bedtime, I made a U-turn and headed for the porch where the women were telling stories and trading recipes, which beats a bad football game any day. TV and radio have been accused of delivering the death blow to conversation, but some of the latest technology has rejuvenated it. Now after pressing a single "stop-and-record" button, you can quietly speak face-to-face and not miss any of the show you've been watching.

A country uncle of mine used to say, "If you're speakin', you ain't larnin'." Given his colorful speech deficiencies, I've always thought he used silence as an excuse not to "larn." Still, he reminds me of the tragically taciturn farmer who at his wife's funeral said, "I loved her so, I almost told her."

The British coffeehouses of the seventeenth and eighteenth centuries were dubbed "penny universities" by those who couldn't afford Oxford or Cambridge. Unlike Starbucks University with its free Wi-Fi and four-dollar lattes, I imagine one could actually have a conversation in those cheaper institutions. Of course, the reason you rarely hear anyone conversing in a Starbucks is the tablets, smart phones, laptops, and "skull-music" devices many are focused on to the exclusion of others. Call me *démodé*, but when my wife or a friend has gone to all the trouble of preparing me a meal, I feel an obligation to give something back. I'm not speaking of clearing the dirty dishes either. I approach most tables with a few memorized talking points, cartoons, photographs, anecdotes, indeed anything that I think my hostess will enjoy. Timing is crucial, however: one should not start too soon.

The first book I read in English 101 was Erich Fromm's *The Art of Loving* in which he convinced me that the essence of love is charity. While tangible gifts may be appreciated and even needed, a house would soon burst if a non-cooking husband like me brought his wife a gift at every meal. What he can give, as Fromm says, is his sincere interest or humor. However, I soon learned by watching brows furl and unfurl that a guest should not overshare.

The old rule of discourse, "Is it true, kind, or needed?" sadly eliminates fiction, gentle sarcasm, and irony from the speech of friends who understand a wink the way our grandchildren understand emoji. Socrates's mother was reported to be a midwife who taught her son to conceive, gestate, and deliver a conversation. Asking a stranger at a cocktail party, "Do you hunt your own truffles or hire a pig," as Jean McClatchy suggested, may give birth to a dialogue, but you may be forced to abort.

In March of 2014, the web satirist Zach Galifianakis scored an interview with President Barack Obama. Apparently thinking he was interviewing Calvin Coolidge, Galifianakis tried to draw the President out by asking, "What is it like to be the last black President?" Said the first African-American to occupy the Oval Office, "Seriously? What is it like for this to be the last time you ever talk to a President?" Satire or not, some decorum must be maintained if conversation is to survive.

I'm unclear why this simple lesson in respect is so hard to learn. On August 2, 1999, *Newsweek* reported that Dr. Michael Brooks, author of *Instant Rapport*, had argued with a flight attendant. Said the psychologist to his perceived social inferior, "Who the fuck do you think you are?" As the conflict escalated, the plane's pilot made an emergency landing, and Brooks, who has advised thousands on how to relate to strangers, was escorted off the plane.

I learned long ago that bull sessions are the students' capstone seminar, and after-supper talk is the cordial. Native Americans in the Northwest still use the "talking stick" to insure that every tribal council member has a chance to speak. Though the stick can limit spontaneity, it's not a bad idea, and it may be passed to the next person if one does not wish to use its authority. What it prevents is the sort of thing one sees among a group of talking heads on television: several people speaking at once in a babel of voices.

A good way to avoid the dead air any conversation is susceptible to is to paraphrase what you've just heard: "So, what you're saying is…." That crutch gives the original speaker a chance to clarify what's been said, and the others time to formulate a rebuttal or amplification. Like most women, my wife and daughter don't have a dead-air problem; however, my son and I do. To correct the awkwardness, we often take a Frisbee outdoors where we can focus on the throw and catch. That way we can talk in our own rhythm without the pressure that chatty women and self-consciousness exert. The essayist Roger Rosenblatt has written that he likes the silences in a game of catch. Indeed, the silences are pleasant as when I'm engrossed in making a salad and my wife is quietly stir-frying some vegetables, but I like the way a Frisbee refocuses the conversation permitting masks to fall and vocal cords to relax.

※

When a close friend in his adolescence suspected he was gay, he asked his very busy father one night if they could talk. The father said, "Not now, Jimmy, I'm too tired. We're going fishing Sunday afternoon; we'll talk then." So James bit his tongue and held it until they were out on Lake Hartwell, the bait was cut, and both lines were in the water. At last the son said, "Dad, I've been wondering…"

"Not now, Jimmy," said his father, "you'll spook the fish."

Ten years later, James came home one weekend from a business trip to tell his wife and his father he was gay. His mother had suspected the truth but avoided that conversation for nearly thirty years.

The Emperor Is Naked: Deconstructionism

On October 11, 2004, I read a longish obituary of Jacques Derrida, the famed French deconstructionist critic who had generated tsunamis in the literary world's tea cup for the past three decades. At the end of the article, the *New York Times'* writer opted to give his readers a sample of Derrida's prose to illustrate a key idea from one of his final interviews collected in *Philosophy in a Time of Terror* (University of Chicago Press, 2003):

> We do not in fact know what we are saying or naming in this way: September 11, *le 11 septembre*, September 11. The brevity of the appellation (September 11, 9/11) stems not only from an economic or rhetorical necessity. The telegram of this metonymy—a name, a number—points out the unqualifiable by recognizing that we do not recognize or even cognize, that we do not yet know how to qualify, that we do not know what we are talking about.

Though I feared that Derrida had finally (in the words of Hobbes of *Calvin and Hobbes*) "made language a complete impediment to understanding," I asked a colleague who teaches literary theory for a loan of the full text thinking that a little more context might be helpful. It wasn't. The *Times'* journalist had chosen well; he was not to blame for the stuttering repetitions, forced humor, fractured syntax, and other infelicities in Derrida any more than Derrida was responsible for what seems to me the denotative clarity of "9-11." Indeed, the term is so popular and expressive that it was chosen by the American Dialect Association as its "Word of the Year" in 2001. A Google search in November of 2005 turned up 85,100,000 hits, and by September 2011, this number had risen to 555,000,000. This six-fold increase should surprise no one given that the wars in Afghanistan and Iraq, two bitterly fought presidential elections, and the high-profile rebuilding in Washington and New York have kept the term on the cusp of our collective memory lobe over the last decade.

Assisting in our recall efforts is the coincidental fact that 911 is the country's emergency telephone number. I'd love to know if the date was chosen by the terrorists for its anxiety-laden connotations, but to the best of my knowledge, it wasn't, nor was it chosen because the number eleven resembled the Twin Towers. (See snopes.com for more in this rich vein.) Intentional or not, the term quickly picked up associations of horror in the West even as it became a rallying cry in many Muslim communities sympathetic to Al Qaeda. Of course, for many conservatives and a few militant liberals like me, it became a call to common action here as well. "9-11" to many of us was as clear a reason to go to war as any in history. Afghanistan, at least, was no War of Jenkins's Ear; Iraq was another story.

Before dismissing Derrida's objections as the uninformed ramblings of a foreign speaker, I decided to ask a class of mostly senior English majors to recast in their own words and comment on the passage above while I did the same myself. Here's my own paraphrase: The world refers to the terrorist attacks and the resulting loss of some three thousand lives in New York, Washington, and Pennsylvania on September 11, 2001 as "9-11." A natural desire for economy and effectiveness of expression is the main reason we have adopted it. But the truncated and somewhat cryptic term reveals our inability to ever know and characterize both what happened on that fateful day and why. Indeed, we do not know what we are talking about when we use "9-11."

Everyone in my class of thirty thought that Derrida had the denotation of "9-11" correct, and half agreed with his implied accusations: namely that "9-11" is "inadequate," "premature," "emotionless," "vague," and, in one case, "a rank euphemism." One student thought the term had convinced a majority of Americans to go to war, accusing the Bush administration of turning "9-11" into a "shrill jingoistic cry" like "Remember the Maine," or, "Remember the Alamo." But one shouldn't blame the term for the way it is used or misused. There's nothing intrinsic in "9-11" (or for that matter "the Holocaust" and "Pearl Harbor") that lends itself to manipulation or distortion. To me the denotation is abundantly clear; connotations naturally and inevitably will vary. But saying that "9-11" is inherently a war cry is like blaming "Christmas" and "the 4th of July" for implying commercialism and pomposity respectively. In the latter case, the blame belongs solely to those bandstand orators over the last two hundred years who have let their love of country cloud their better judgment.

According to one student, Derrida's chief objection to "9-11" was its prematurity: "we adopted this term without due consideration," she thought. When this point was discussed in class, I said that people of all cultures traditionally name the baby at birth or shortly thereafter. In some societies, people get a new name after an initiation or confirmation, but the new name may need adjustments, and the old is seldom discarded without regret. Indeed, "9-11" might change if there's a larger tragedy on some future September 11th the way "The Great War" became "World War I" in the 1940s as fifty-five million lay dead or dying. Personally, I cannot fault anyone for quickly adopting the term. Effective discourse demanded that we name it something; we did, it stuck, and it's not going away. Can 555,000,000 usages all be wrong?

As for "9-11" being "a rank euphemism," I'd have to disagree as well. There are circumlocutions and there are roundabout expressions, but in the worst sense ("guestage" for "hostage"), euphemisms are criminally evasive, subterfuges that seek to obscure something offensive or false for all the wrong reasons. (Recall, for example, Adolf Eichmann saying at his trial that he was "an expert on migration problems.") Personally, I find no felonious intent in "9-11." Had we dubbed the tragedy "Bush's Blooper," we would have deserved all the scorn we surely would have received. It's possible the tragedy might have been called "World Trade Center" or "WTC" or "Ground Zero" tying the tragedy to the place rather than the time, but "9-11" has a natural trochaic rhythm that "WTC" lacks. Plus the latter ignores what happened in Washington and Pennsylvania. Should the term allude to the mangled bodies more directly? In fact, "Bloody Tuesday" has been used 6,430 times according to Google in connection with "9-11"—a far cry from 555,000,000.

As for the term being shortened to a fault, I would remind these critics of Zipf's Law and point them to Maya Lin's Viet Nam War Memorial in Washington, DC especially now juxtaposed as it is with that affectation of grandeur, the World War II Monument, across the Mall. The understatement of Lin's triangular slabs of black marble plowing their way to a halt in some of this nation's most hallowed ground is possibly the most moving memorial ever created. Few who have visited it have left dry eyed. What better way to commemorate the dead in a war that

America lost than inscribe the names of the 58,000 fallen on a figurative instrument of frustration and hopelessness? "9-11" has the same poignant simplicity with its overtones of a fumbled emergency call while a loved one lies gasping at the caller's feet.

One student who disagreed with Derrida's brusque dismissal of "9-11" thought it was a haiku, a rough stone dropped into the well of her consciousness that brought up reminders of the New York firemen, the leadership of Mayor Guiliani, Al Qaeda, and the continuing threat of terrorist attack. A longer more descriptive "poem," the student felt, probably would not have had the richness this simple time reference has.

One of her classmates thought that while the metonymy the world has taken to heart and mind cannot represent the full horror of the day, "What more can we do? We communicate with signs and symbols all the time, and if we are careful, we are successful more often than not." I agree. Walker Percy pointedly observed that the deconstructionist is one who charges language with the inability to communicate but leaves a phone message for his wife to bring home a pepperoni pizza. If the critic's wife brings home the pizza requested, who can sincerely argue that language is "radically indeterminate." Isn't Derrida left with mozzarella in his mustache?

Does language ever fail us? Of course it does. Recall the postcard writer who wrote, "The scenery is here; wish you were beautiful." Or June Cleaver's famous command to her husband, "Ward, come upstairs and talk to the Beaver." Or this sign announcing the opening of a new business, "Owned and Operated by a Clemson Grad and Formal CU Footbal Player." Or this classified ad advertising a house for sale, "Brick, hardwood floors; this one won't last." Or this sentence from the *Fresno Bee*, "The new taxes will put debt-ridden Massachusetts back in the African-American." Or finally, George W. Bush saying on Oct. 18, 2004, "September the 4th, 2001, I stood in the ruins of the Twin Towers. It's a day I will never forget."

⚘

To Derrida's claim that a text means nothing or so many things that it's meaningless, and to the fundamentalist's claim that a text has a single literal meaning, the New Critics might say as Laurence Perrine once argued, "A text may mean many things, not all of them." As an old New Critic, that places me squarely in the middle, which is where Aristotle said virtue resides. Post-modern theorists like Derrida have been described by their detractors as "gulls in a trawler's wake" or "eunuchs in a harem." Derrida's paragraph at the start of this essay is a long, unhappy way from John Crowe Ransom's definition, "[A critic is] one who in dealing with a work of art creates a little work of art in its honor."

Ransom's ideal is so lofty it makes me a bit dizzy, so my model is a bit more pragmatic: it's the work of a scholar like Dr. Matthew Bruccoli formerly of the University of South Carolina, one of whose specialties is American literature in the Jazz Age. I recall approaching him once when I was in graduate school about a problem I was having with a passage in *The Great Gatsby*. My question was whether the Montenegrin *Orderi de Danilo* medal that Gatsby claimed he was awarded in The Great War would have been inscribed in English. Professor Bruccoli smiled as he reached in his pocket and to my astonishment pulled out one of the rare Montenegrin medals he'd recently purchased at auction.

He then pointed out that on his medal and all others like it there is no inscription because it is coated with a ceramic glaze which cannot be engraved. Now that's the sort of clarity and authority I expect from a critic!

For myself, I shall seek aid from critics and scholars of Bruccoli's caliber until Jacques Derrida and his disciples can give me definitive answers without brushing me off saying language and art can only approximate reality. We know that. And I shall abide by the words of Ernest Hemingway in *A Farewell to Arms*, "There were many words that you could not stand to hear and finally only the names of places had dignity. Certain numbers were the same way and certain dates and these with the names of places were all you could say and have them mean anything. Abstract words such as *glory, honor, courage*, or *hallow* were obscene beside the concrete names of villages, the numbers of roads, the names of rivers, the numbers of regiments and the dates." Did you hear that Professor Derrida? "Certain dates...were all you could say and have them mean anything."

> [A fuller version of this essay was published in *The Vocabula Review*, May 2006 and is available in the magazine's archives.]

Caviar vs. Roe: Definitions

A definition builds a word wall around the wilderness of an idea.—
paraphrase of Samuel Butler

"We are not terrorists. We are jihadists, and jihad is not terrorism."
—*Ramy Zamzam*

For several years, I've had a photograph of Samuel Johnson in my study, not so much out of recognition of what Dr. Johnson knew and wrote, but for what he didn't know and his willingness to admit it. After attributing "sagacity, faithfulness and even understanding" to the "largest of all quadrupeds," he described among other things the elephant's sexual activity on the impeccable authority of his imagination. "In copulation," Johnson wrote, "the female receives the male lying upon her back; and such is his [modesty], that he never covers the female so long as anyone is in sight." Of course, the latter might be said of all wild mammals, for when mating, they are not so much shy as vulnerable. To the best of my knowledge, no one ever challenged Johnson's elephantine definition the way one woman took exception to "pastern," which Johnson had defined as the knee of the horse instead of the ankle. When asked how this error might have occurred, Johnson replied, "Ignorance, madam, pure ignorance."

When it comes to definitions, as my father used to say, "Skipper knows his way around ignorance." When introducing me to his military friends, he would occasionally recall that in high school I had defined "pyromaniac" as "one who enjoys sitting by the fire." He'd then pause and say, "He compounded the problem by illustrating the word as follows, 'After the round-up, all the pyromaniacs enjoyed sitting around the campfire singing "Home on the Range."

If he'd had a drum, he might have added a rimshot. My English teacher was more merciful. She granted me partial credit for the reference to fire, but of course my shot in the dark missed not only the boat but the harbor as well.

With well over a hundred dictionaries on my shelves today, I have acquired a local reputation as an "ento-etymologist," or a "debugger of words." Unfortunately, reputations are like Jayne Mansfield's breasts: many want to squeeze them to see if they are deserved. Not long ago, a retired professor of chemistry asked me to define "'substantivity' as it differs from 'affinity'." I blanched having never heard "substantivity" before, but I manned up, admitted the gap in my education, and promised to do an on-line search because *American Heritage*, the only dictionary on hand, did not list it. When I put the word in Google, I discovered that the fellow who'd sent me on this quest had defined both words at some length in a textbook he'd written fifteen years earlier. As a result, I have so little affinity for "substantivity" I won't bother to define it. I sent him the link and have not heard a substantive word since.

Now "*mokusatsu*" is another kettle of fish, and I'm not talking *fugu*, but it's just as dangerous. It seems that "*mokusatsu*" can mean "ignore" or "no comment" to a speaker of Japanese; the word depends on the company it keeps. Thus in July of 1945, when Prime Minister Suzuki left a cabinet discussion of the Potsdam Ultimatum, the minister used this shifty word in a coy sentence meant to imply that his administration had not decided whether to accept the Allies' surrender terms. Tragically, the opposite was reported to Harry Truman, and shortly thereafter, the first atomic bomb was ordered for Hiroshima. In the best of all possible worlds, Suzuki should have chosen his words more carefully in speaking to the press especially after diplomatic relations had been severed. Moreover, the White House should have checked the translation they'd received from the Domei News Agency before killing 100,000 people, mostly civilians and Korean prisoners.

Mokusatsu is a "contranym," a word which can mean one thing as well as its opposite. The clearest example I know of in English is "dust." If, for example, I overhear my short-tempered neighbor giving her Mexican maid the order, "Dust!" I have no idea whether the employee is being instructed to dust the living room or dust some tomato plants for aphids. In other words, I don't know if the dust is coming off or going on, so the dictionary is no help. Only context will solve the problem because lexicographers are no more omniscient than the gods.

Dr. Johnson called words the *"primum materium"* (I'd argue for phonemes), but without definition and context, the reader or listener is lost in space filled with static. Take "juice" for example. With that word as my wife and I use it, neither dictionary nor context will help the uninitiated because it's a "family word" exclusive to us. For years, our children struggled to pronounce the German *"Tschüss,"* so it deteriorated into "juice," and it means "bye," "toodeloo," or *"ciao."* If a non-German speaker heard my wife say "Juice!" as I crossed the kitchen threshold, I imagine he'd think she wanted me to pick up some orange juice on the way home, but he'd be mistaken. It's just our liminal farewell honed by fifty years of wedlock.

Like words, definitions are not tube socks: one size does not fit all feet. Indeed, meanings are more like Imelda Marcos's shoes. Here are a few of the "styles" currently available:

- The dialectal: *yawl*—"a Southern sailboat"

73

(Anonymous)
- The proverbial: *futility*—"two bald men fighting over a comb" (Russian proverb)
- The quotable: *family*—"the we of me" (Carson McCullers)
- The humorous: *cosmetics*—"crease paint" (Raymond Cvikota)
- The cynical: *alone*—" in bad company" (Ambrose Bierce)
- The circular: *courtesy*—"being courteous" (Anonymous)
- The reciprocating: *typhoon*—"a hurricane in the Eastern hemisphere and a typhoon in the West" (Anonymous)
- The obscure: *net*—"anything reticulated or decussated at equal distances, with interstices between the intersections" (Samuel Johnson)
- The ostensive: *red*—"defining this color solely by pointing to red objects—apples, stop signs, roses [etc.]..." (Wikipedia)

So, what's it going to be: insane or eccentric, savage or aboriginal inhabitant, illegal immigrant or pioneer, terrorist or freedom fighter, hit man or well-regulated militiaman, war or annexation, unborn babe or fetus, law or theory? As these pairings imply, a great many of the issues that confront us today can be reduced to defining the terms, and to the better definer go the spoils. During the Cold War, another pair of a different sort that received a lot of attention was capitalism and socialism. Since that conflict is closer to resolution than the others above, I'll finish briefly with it. In 1985, the editors of the *Oxford English Dictionary* granted lexicographers in the former Soviet Union the rights to publish a Russian edition of the *OED*. In the small print, however, the British editors relinquished any oversight of the finished product. As a result, capitalism

was defined as "an economic and social system based on…
the exploitation of man by man." And socialism emerged as,
"a system which is replacing capitalism." As the Cold War's
conclusion proved the Russian definitions false, capitalism
as well as democracy have gained a clear but sometimes
ragged edge. Of course, those definitions did not *cause* the
Kremlin's failure, but they were some of the termites in the
foundation.

How Many Lords, My Lump?
The Sweetness of Error

"Every night is the dawn of a new error." —*Anonymous*

"A man's errors are his portals of discovery." —*James Joyce*

Anatole France preferred "the errors of enthusiasm to the indifference of wisdom." Vilfredo Pareto wrote, "Give me a fruitful error any time, full of seeds, bursting with its own corrections. You can keep your sterile truths for yourself." And Ortega y Gasset felt, "Man's real treasure is the treasure of his mistakes, piled up stone by stone through thousands of years." Indifferent wisdom and sterile truths notwithstanding, one may die eating the *Amanita virosa* identified as "safe" in the 1991 color edition of the *Petit Larousse Dictionary*.

Of course there are errors, and there are errors. In 1995, a legislative comma printed as a hyphen eliminated thousands of Indian Gowaris from affirmative-action benefits. Following that clerical error, 113 Gowaris died in what was intended as a peaceful protest. About twenty years earlier, Dr. Hayward Foy was indicted on forty-two charges of selling the amphetamine phendimetrizine. But when Foy's lawyers pointed out that the Illinois legal code had spelled the drug *pheudimetrizine*, all charges were dismissed—the code had the drug misspelled, an error that had been corrected in 1975.

When Kirby Olson wrote that "to err [is] divine," he was surely not thinking of how one word led to the tragic conclusion of World War II and set the stage for another. More likely, he had in mind some inspired slips of the mind like the "Perishing Rifles," "World War Too," and

"Catch-1984." The realm of student errors is a kaleidoscopic thicket where Mother Teresa achieves "St. Hood," bankers seek the "Notary Republic," Jesus is interrogated by "Poncho Pilate," and drug addicts kill for "morpheme tablets." In this alternate universe, "Bach has twenty kids and practices on a spinster in the attic," villanelles are "bad girls," American soldiers die in "Indigo-China," Euripides produces "Media," Moses creates "mosaics," and "The Jabberwocky" is written by Carol Lewis. Most students disappear from professors' lives after they drop off their final examinations, but one young man I taught stayed in the area and opened a bicycle shop not far from Clemson. I had a good mind to take my bike to his establishment until I read his newspaper ad: "...Bike Shop: owned & operated by a Clemson Grad & formal CU footbal player." Formal as this announcement was, I wasn't going to trust my Shimano derailleur to one unable to spell "football" after playing the game for four years at a university that aspires to be worthy of its athletic department.

But what are the young to do when so much of the culture is in error to start with? Aesop's story of the ant and the grasshopper is an elementary case in point. Ask any entomologist, and she will tell you that grasshoppers are as diligent about feeding themselves as ants, most of which are torpid through the winter in the middle latitudes. In health classes, students are often told of the "funny bone" which is a nerve and the "jugular vein" which is an artery. In history, the story of Nero "fiddling" while Rome burned is likewise seldom examined as it should be. Indeed, no fiddle or violin existed during the Roman Empire; what Nero probably played was a small lyre called a *fidicula*, thus the "fiddling." In their English classes, students may learn that the lion is "the king of the jungle," but if they take German, they'll learn that it's "the king of the desert." Both languages have it wrong, of course; lions dominate the African plains.

Normally I'm the sort to note that two wrongs don't make a right, but three rights make a left. I also have a habit of scouring errata lists for, you guessed it, errors. When I was teaching full-time, I used to peruse the footnotes in the new anthologies publishers mailed out for review. I'll never forget one gloss of an allusion to "the fraudulent Contrivances of Plagius" in an essay Ben Franklin wrote at age sixteen. The footnote explained that the reference was "a pun on Pelagius, an early British theologian whose belief in free will was attacked by Calvinists and Puritans." But this made no sense since the young Deist was a staunch defender of free will. The allusion was simply to the fraudulent contrivances of plagiarists, who transcribed the work of others to embellish their own as Franklin clearly states in a later passage.

When I first started teaching interdisciplinary humanities courses, I made so many errors that I made a *mea culpa* session at the start of most classes a regular feature. But my most embarrassing public error was made when my wife and I took a basic computer class in the late 1980s. A Clemson instructor stood at a lectern while about a dozen of us sat facing him and our new computers. After telling us where the on-off switch was, he said, "Now type 'Are you in?'" I did as instructed figuring this was some silly personified DOS code to waken the computer genie from his nap, who if "in" would fetch something called my "electronic mail." When my screen suddenly appeared different from the students around me, the instructor walked around to see what the problem was. "No, no," he said, barely able to contain himself, "Type R-U-N."

Perhaps the most famous English literary error is

Cortez's "discovery" of the Pacific in Keats's "On First Looking into Chapman's Homer." As English teachers never tire of pointing out, it was not "stout Cortez"; it was "fat Balboa." What I have long found interesting in this regard is that Keats's friend Cowden Clark immediately pointed out the mistake, yet the poet did not correct the error in any edition while he lived. Some readers have theorized that he was alluding to Cortez's being the first to view the Valley of Mexico, vast as a sea. Others have thought "Balboa" spoiled the rhythm, but it doesn't, especially if the superfluous "stout" is dropped. No, I say; sly John Keats knew that a rich error had much longer legs than the truth, or I would not be writing about it almost two hundred years later.

Rectal-Cranial Transfers: Euphemisms

"I was an expert on migration problems." —*Adolf Eichmann*

"Death and genitals are things that frighten people, and when people are frightened, they develop means of concealment and aggression. It is common sense." —*Noam Chomsky*

Sterling Silver grew up reading Webster's edition of the Bible in which Onan doesn't "spill his seed"; he "frustrates his purpose." After the boy's father mysteriously died in prison, Sterling's mother mumbled something about "a platform collapsing at a state function." But Sterling's odd linguistic habit began at the Search and Rescue Seminary where he started calling Devil's food cake "Salvation Chocolate." As a freshman, he defied the "Prince of Insufficient Light" and announced, "Sam Hill is a place for those who don't believe in the Lawdy." By the time he was a junior, however, he was swearing freely: "Well, I swan!" was commonly heard in the dorm, and at football games, he was known to yell, "Cheese and rice, ref!" When his girlfriend Mary moved on, he exclaimed, "H-e-double-hockey-sticks—she can go to heckfire and tarnation for all I care." Privately, Mary explained that Sterling had "had his bell rung" playing intramurals and was a "terminally Caucasian male" on the dance floor. In his exit interview, Sterling told the dean of men that "sweet zombie Jebus" had lost his appeal.

Of course, Sterling was never one to call a spade a spade when he could call it a "vulpine-refuge evacuator." So the next stop was the US Army where he was issued a pair of "leather personnel carriers" and an "aerodynamic personnel decelerator" because Sterling had said he wanted to go airborne. He actually wrote that he wanted to join the "vertical transportation corps," but his commanding officer said the army had no need for elevator operators. After basic training, Sterling qualified for Officer Candidate School where he learned about "enhanced radiation weapons," "sunshine units," and huge Russian missiles aimed at our "factors of peace." He also heard a lecture on how the change from "War Department" to "Department of Defense" had been worth billions to the military. Because of his "communicatory jujitsu skills," Sterling was sent to the Pentagon as a speech writer in the same office that gave us "Manifest Destiny" for killing Native Americans and "Post Traumatic Stress Disorder" for the mental health of those who survived the horrors of Viet Nam. "Just three wars ago," Sterling wrote his mother, "'PTSD' was 'shell shock.' From two syllables to eight, a 200% gain in less than a century—now that's progress."

In his first job, Sterling was asked to "ethicate" spending $2043 for a $.13 steel nut. Explained the speech writer, "If you call it a 'hexiform rotatable surface compression unit,' the taxpayer's nethermost aperture is proactively greased."

As his reputation grew, Sterling moved over to Langley to fabricate phrases for the CIA like "collateral damage" and "terminate with extreme prejudice." Life was good until he described the bullet hole in Ronald Reagan's chest as a "ballistically induced aperture in the subcutaneous environment." When asked by the *Washington Post* to confirm the report that he'd written so callously, Sterling said that was a "categorical inaccuracy," but he soon "underwent a career adjustment" for speaking with "incomplete candor."

Out of work with little in the bank, Sterling was desperate. He wrote his mother that he was suffering from "illness and fatigue," but the truth was his boss was sick and tired of him. In a job interview, he claimed he'd "implemented a massive office reorganization" at the Pentagon, but a phone call revealed that he'd merely moved some file cabinets while he was awaiting his security clearance. Eventually he landed a job selling "experienced furs" as a "retail therapist," but he lost that when his "turf accountant" demanded a payment on his gambling debt. His girlfriend, Linda, owner of "a capital-intensive, female-empowerment club," found him a job driving a "motorized transportation module," but he lost that as well in a fight with a "petroleum transfer engineer."

It was about that time that Sterling fell hard for "Jane Plain." Her litany of "swamps" that used to be "wetlands" and "trees" that were "reforestation units" inexplicably resonated with him. The purity and directness of her language made him tremble. Was there ever a time, he wondered, when "dental appliances" were "false teeth," "daytime dramas" were "soaps," "running shoes" were "sneakers," and "the landfill" just "a dump"? Sterling never learned the answer, for when he referred to one of Jane's "barking spiders" as a "fart," she marched off without pageantry.

After a few months on a District of Columbia "correctional campus" for a "wardrobe malfunction," he was released. But not before he'd learned "footwear maintenance engineering" which led him to the arms of "Mustang Sally," an "unclaimed blessing" and fellow bootblack. The two moved to the "Georgetown arrondissement" just a few blocks from his parole officer's home.

Sally, now Sterling's "spouse equivalent," was a former ad writer for Spin, Polish, and English. It was she who gave us "adorable" for "small," "the other white meat" for "pork," "dried plums" for "prunes," "huggable" for "fat," "underarm wetness" for "sweat," and "occasional irregularity" for "constipation." She lost her job, however, when she ran a "Haul derriere" ad for Mercedes in the *Wall Street Journal*.

Living on government cheese under the Key Street Bridge and unable to afford "portable hydration" or "interdental stimulators," Sterling had never been happier. For years he'd patronized "Linda's House of Negotiable Affection," but now he was ready to "embrace the connubial couch." One night, however, as Sally was heating Sterling's "ball-park bratwurst," she sensed something was not right. Eventually, our protagonist admitted he'd been feral so long he wanted to retain the right to conduct "postnuptial research." Chastened but unreformed, Sally left for an "optional swimsuit area" on the Potomac. The last anyone heard, she had volunteered to teach a "Gut and Butt" class if the proprietor changed the name to "Abs and Glutes."

Within days of Sally's departure, Sterling's curious speech habit made a 180° turn. Oleomargarine which for decades had been "I Can't Believe It's Not Butter," turned to "axle grease." The newspapers he slept under became "dead-tree editions," the lottery he'd played morphed into "a tax on idiots," and while his weak chin was still a "confident overbite," his mouth was a "pie hole." Lost within the Beltway, Sterling wasn't "probing alternative *termini*"; he was "investigating hopeless destinations."

Looking at what had become "a Victorian loveseat tuber," Sterling realized he had "suboptimized his potential." He went, therefore, to visit an "afterlife coach" to make arrangements for a "basement apartment," for he knew he was "circling the drain." A few days later, the *Post* reported that Sterling had died of "therapeutic misadventures."

Wrong Turns on Frost's "Road": Interpretation

"I know what I have given you. I do not know what you have received." —*Antonio Porchia*

"[Critics] don't know what the songs mean. Shit, *I* don't know what they mean." —*Bob Dylan*

When I was in graduate school in the 1960s, a couple of my professors would routinely come to class and read their jaundiced notes aloud for the duration. This travesty passed for teaching. Even though a lectern is a piece of classroom furniture etymologically designed to assist a reader, I resolved that I would never read my notes standing behind one. I might read a poem by Dickinson or a few paragraphs of Faulkner, but not my earth-bound commentary on these masters of flight. Toward my personal goal of saying something fresh if not original in each class, I started keeping files on the most essential works I taught, and whenever I found a useful item, I would photocopy it and drop it in the appropriate folder. The purpose was two-fold: to prevent myself from getting bored teaching the canon, however it is defined, and to keep my students interested with the latest research and relevant illustrations available to me.

When I retired from full-time teaching in 2007, I noticed that Frost's "The Road Not Taken" had accumulated a fatter file than most. [To read the poem, click on: http://www.bartleby.com/119/1.html] Among the collected items were student essays, photographs, cartoons, scribbled insights, and misreadings. In one essay, a student told me that her high school chorus had sung the poem as if it were

"Hymn to the Road Less Traveled." The choral director had entirely missed Frost's intention to skewer the sententious narrator.

I also found a black-and-white photograph torn from Pinney and Say's out-of-print poetry text *Two Ways of Seeing*. The editors' visual aid for the poem showed a narrow path diverging from a broad one, yet the poet clearly states the two roads were identical. As the poem's reader soon discovers, a falsehood is already in the making as the narrator imagines the story he will be telling "ages and ages hence." Moreover, the distinction between the narrator's original decision and the way it is remembered is not made clear in the editors' questions that accompany the text. One question reads, "Which path in the photograph might Frost have chosen?" That of course assumes that Frost is the narrator and his options are different. But he's not the narrator, and the options offered in the poem are very similar. In fact, the choices resemble those faced by Buridan's ass: the hay bale on the right, the hay bale on the left, or starvation.

Surely those who most consistently misread the poem are the newspaper cartoonists I read, but then I suspect I read the comic pages more critically than most. In one strip, Ziggy said, "I took the road less traveled, and now I'm totally lost." Zig's neighbor, Frank, in *Frank and Ernest* said, "I took the road less traveled, and now I need a front-end alignment." And Jeff MacNelly's Shoe once said, "I took the road less traveled, and it sure could use some more rest stops." Given the popularity of Frost's catch sentence, "I took the road less traveled," English teachers will have a hard time convincing future students that there was no under-utilized road in the first place. Frank Sinatra's ever popular "I Did It My Way" just complicates matters.

As I neared the back of my folder, I noticed a piece of onionskin that had acquired several accordion creases. Unfolding it, I found the carbon copy of a note describing the first time I had taught the poem. Repressed or forgotten, I'm not sure which, here was a scrap worthy of my own Dead Sea scrolls. As it happened, nearly forty years ago, I was prattling merrily along about the virtues of the road less traveled, when a student raised his hand. "How can there be a less traveled road," he wanted to know, "if both roads are worn 'really about the same?'" Fortunately for me, the bell rang, but the next time the class met, I begged a stunned and now nameless adolescent for a pardon. Had this incident occurred after the introduction of student evaluations, I might never have won tenure. As soon as I realized my error, I went to the library and discovered in Lawrance Thompson's biography of Frost that the poet was poking fun at a fastidious, handwringing friend who rued his inability to bilocate. To my relief, the friend, when he first read the poem, did not recognize himself as the object of Frost's gentle "fooling" as he puts it.

With two grandfathers who claimed that they "walked to school uphill both ways," I knew the hype Frost was satirizing. When I thought of my snap decision to join the Army six months out of high school and my switch from business to English after a stimulating class discussion of *The Lord of the Flies*, I also realized how often key decisions in our lives are made with a mental coin toss. To cross the bridge or burn it, to fish or cut bait, to charge it or pay cash, most of us overcome our initial paralysis despite not having all the information we need. When our decisions bear fruit, we frequently make the story of how we succeeded one of epic, self-aggrandizing proportions: "I, yes I, took the road less traveled, my beamish boy, and that has made me the monumental success who stands before you." As Frost says, we usually tell these tall tales with a sigh of regret to audibly underscore how steep that hill was and how mightily we struggled to reach the summit.

I'm not sure *The New Yorker's* Donald Reilly had "The Road Not Taken" in mind, but in one masterful cartoon, he shows five pre-adolescent boys sitting around a campfire. The oldest presciently says, "Someday when we're old, we're going to look back and embellish this." Frost could not have drawn it any better.

When Each Extended Finger Means Something Else: Gestures

"Only Michael Jackson knew exactly what the 'crotch grab' meant, and he's dead." — *The Wordspinner*

"No matter what a woman wears, going commando dramatically increases her body-language fluency." — *The Wordspinner*

Without speech, our ancestors gestured and grunted to communicate for 3.8 million years. It wasn't until the FOXP2 gene mutated about 150,000 years ago, and the larynx relocated itself a little lower in the throat about 30,000 years ago that humans were capable of song.

Some linguists contend that 60% or more of all human communication is still accomplished by nostril flares, curtseys, and other physical gyrations. I've always found that estimate high, but there's no question humans have had far more time to polish their gesticulations than their speech. If I would parachute into an Amazon rain forest, I'm sure most of what I'd communicate to the natives who hauled me from the trees would be via the hands, the face, and the occasional scream. I imagine that kissing the feet of those who save you is universally understood. But if Stephen Hawking cannot use his hands to explain how black holes emit radiation, he can still communicate very effectively to his fellow scientists.

One Amazon tribe raps the skull with the knuckles to signal "mmm-good." The first anthropologist to observe that gesture admits he was puzzled at first, but he soon understood as the context unfolded. Likewise Lewis and Clark crossing the Great Plains quickly learned that two index fingers rising from a brave's forehead meant "buffalo," and one hand cupped behind an ear indicated that the animals could be heard moving at a gallop, which was mimed by the fingers. If these gestures were accompanied by the chief bringing two or three fingers to his lips followed by a puffing sound, the explorers knew he wanted them to smoke the peace pipe before the hunt, mimed by pulling back a bow. And if the chief struck his left palm repeatedly with his right thumb, they knew he expected some form of reimbursement for the pelts his braves would soon collect.

People blind from birth instinctively gesture when they speak, and deaf children spontaneously create a sign language when housed together. The momentum that attaches itself to gesticulating is often seen in Japan and Korea when people bow to their telephone callers. Though Tebowing has come and gone, and while the number of waves and winks has been estimated at close to a million, gestures are remarkably stable unlike their spoken counterparts. Once the Roman emperor began blessing his people with the index and middle fingers of his extended right hand, the popes continued the practice despite centuries of Roman persecution. European kings followed suit to the point that Louis XIV had a silver cast made of his right hand, so he could bless the masses with a comfortable wave of his wand.

In a silent medium like painting, the hands are often the most expressive elements especially when the faces show no emotion. Consider Van Eyck's *Marriage of Arnolfini* in which the stiffness of this arranged marriage is cabled through the hands. The monochromatic groom has raised his right hand as he listens to an oath of fidelity delivered offstage while the other hand, extended to his bride, is as lifeless as a fileted flounder. Meanwhile, the bride has placed her right hand in her husband's with all the passion of that cold fish beneath her. Her left hand has shyly lifted her wedding gown a few inches to reveal some rich fabrics for her parents to see. It seems inevitable that the husband would be unfaithful, and the two would divorce without ever producing any children.

It's well known that bilinguals use more gestures when speaking the weaker of their two languages. Thus, when the second language is love, the hands instinctively come to the tongue's aid as seen in the Arnolfini's double portrait. The State Department schools its employees before posting them to places where a "thumbs up" can convey a "thumbs down." For several months, I worked with a Japanese graduate student in international trade trying to strengthen his English. Another thing I tried to strengthen was his marshmallow handshake, but he was so accustomed to bowing, my lesson went limply unheeded. As Twain used to say about his wife's cursing, the student had "the words without the rhythm."

After he graduated, I began tutoring a young Saudi engineer. Trying to make both of us feel more comfortable as we conversed in my office, I crossed my legs in such a way that he was looking at the soles of my shoes. This display I learned is insulting, but he graciously accepted my apology. He said that many of his professors do the same thing, so he figured it was a cultural difference of little consequence. Fortunately, there was no press coverage.

Humans are born gesturing, and sometimes it's the last thing we do. A man who killed his two children after his wife filed for divorce was hanged. A review of the gallows video revealed that the condemned died while giving his ex-wife the finger with both barrels.

A century after Galileo's death in a related case, his body was exhumed, needless to say, without his consent. In a mortuary, the three bones of one middle finger were laid end to end, wired together, and placed in a glass reliquary. The finger, a posthumous quotation and part of the exhibit at Florence's Museo Galileo, is pointed directly at the Vatican.

Except for poker tells, one largely unexplored category of gesture is the unconscious variety. When a colleague was telling some friends at lunch about his recent heart attack, he brought his fingertips together in a gesture known as steepling. This is usually done sitting down in the presence of social inferiors and essentially says, "I'm better than you." But when Charlie began to describe his brush with death, his hands began to pulsate like a healthy heart. When I asked him about it in the parking lot, he said he never steepled.

Finally, there are the spontaneous gestures of man and nature. When the moon eclipsed Clemson's view of the sun several years ago, crickets could be heard at two in the afternoon while thousands of pale crescents danced under the trees, for nature has her own repertoire. As the moon continued its passage, the sun reappeared to a round of applause, and several of us reached skyward to embrace the warmth.

※

When a platoon of Chinese soldiers mooned a crowd of Russian border observers during the Cold War, relations between the two countries took a turn for the worse. Thus when students ask how to succeed in graduate school, I recommend they keep their pants zipped and try some calculated nodding. First, I say, sign up for classes your first semester that you know you're going to like. Then, sit near the front of the class, smile, take notes, and nod agreeably when the professor looks at you. Don't overdo it, but a few sage gestures can turn a professor into a mentor.

The Gestapo vs. the Antinomians: Grammar

"Grammar rules are banana peels on the sidewalk of life."—
Anonymous

"Grammar is the art of putting language in its place on or off the sidewalk."—*Anonymous*

For over a thousand years, Old, Middle, and Modern English flourished without a grammar book to their names. King Alfred, Chaucer, and Shakespeare relied solely on their exquisitely tuned ears because Fowler, Strunk, White, and their kin had not yet been born.

In the fifteenth century when grammarians were gaining a beachhead in Europe, the Holy Roman Emperor Sigismund declared, "I am the Roman Emperor, and I am above grammar." With little Latin and less Greek, Sigismund was from the same school as George W. Bush who blithely assumed that imprecision in language carried few if any consequences. *A Short Introduction to English Grammar*, the first of its kind, was published in 1762 by Bishop Robert Lowth, but the powdered-wig rules he cobbled were more relevant to Latin than English. Is it any wonder then that grammar reminds many of a forbidding classical façade? To satirize the idea in 1802 that language etiquette is the lace doily on a rococo couch, pretty but inessential, Timothy Dexter added a page of commas to his unpunctuated autobiography with instructions that readers could "peper and solt them as they plese[.]"

Freelance grammarian Dexter reminds me of the senior who said she placed a comma in a text when she needed to breathe. She lectured me after I failed one of her essays for a score of comma splices and fragments saying, "If you get hung up on whether it's 'the yolk is white' or 'the yolk are white,' you're likely to overlook the fact that the yolk is yellow." I accused her of being a loose cannon from the Breathitarian Armory, but her point was well taken: it is the content, not the comma, that we read for.

In *Building a Bridge to the Eighteenth Century* (1999), Neil Postman reminds readers that grammar comprised a third of the medieval Trivium, and that curricular prominence has carried over to the present. Among logic and rhetoric, grammar, he argues, is the "least potent, the least able to help students do what we call critical thinking.... Indeed," he says, "it is difficult to know why grammar, as it is presently taught, is included in the curriculum at all." That subordinate clause "as it is presently taught" presents a stumbling block for many teachers of writing because Postman cannot know how thousands of us teach the subject. He apparently thinks it is taught prescriptively by completing exercises in a workbook without any extended reading or writing involved. However, judging from the teachers I've interviewed, none at the college level uses this Gradgrindian method exclusively.

Moreover, Postman's point about the relative "impotence" of grammar is overstated. My experience has demonstrated that proofreading for grammar errors after the first or second draft helps to insure that the sentences follow logically and are phrased to make the argument persuasive. In other words, grammar is a partner of logic and rhetoric, not extraneous. Take any clause like "all men are created equal" in the Gettysburg Address and forge a subject-verb disagreement on top of a misspelling. Now imagine how quickly that logical and rhetorical masterpiece would have dropped from our national memory if Lincoln had written, "All mens is equal."

The ideal, as I view it from behind the lectern, is for students to read vast quantities of great literature, discuss it, write about it, and absorb the grammar by osmosis. Alas, that rarely happens. To be sure, there are readers like Joseph Conrad who grow up on Polish, and then "picked up" English like a penny in the parking lot by reading Shakespeare and Dickens. Such student readers are as rare as black tulips. In my own case, I gathered rudiments of grammar reading The Hardy Boys series, but learned even more in formal terms by diagramming sentences and completing work sheets in high school. I never had a grammar course *per se* in college, but I did correct the mistakes my professors had marked on my papers and rewrote the corrected sentences as directed.

The place I really learned my subject was the classroom in which I had to teach it. The week before entering that class was the first time I'd read a grammar the way I'd been taught to read a poem by the New Critics: with a dictionary by my side and an eye to tracking the antecedent of every pronoun. I was also terrified some kid from a fancy prep school was going to ask me why I had not used a possessive before a gerund. So it behooved me to learn what gerunds were, and reading Faulkner was no help in that regard. Grammar gave me the technical language I could use to help a student pinpoint a problem. If you've ever been on the receiving end of, "That doesn't sound right," you know it's not much help.

Faced with widespread indifference, I began to wonder how best to motivate undergraduates to learn the ground rules of language. One way I discovered, and it's only one, involves bringing to class language issues that have immediate consequences. An example I used in January of 2010 involved Sen. Harry Reid's innocent use of "Negro."

Despite his long advocacy of civil rights, many of his opponents called for Reid's resignation even when the latest US Census form listed "Negro" as a racial category that African Americans may choose to identify themselves. If nothing else, the class discussion emphasized that word choice often has seismic repercussions in the public arena. I understood that best when a friend with eighteen years of "superior academic service," according to one of her superiors, lost her job for using one ill-considered word.

Another fine classroom example is the now famous sentence Sarah Palin used in her last speech as Alaska's governor in 2009: "It is as throughout all Alaska that big wild good life teeming along the road that is north to the future." After writing Palin's sentence on the board, I asked the students to paraphrase it. As we attempted to read the governor's mind ("Are there moose in those woods?" one young man wanted to know), many, I think, understood why writing or speech of such ludicrous ineptitude may become a lightning rod. Another student typed Palin's sentence on his laptop, but Microsoft did not issue a single green or red squiggle. The day has not arrived when we can rely on a grammar checker app.

To detractors like Thoreau ("Any fool can make a rule, and every fool will mind it."), a red-penciled grammar error is the equivalent of denying a soldier his weekend pass based on a loose thread: a cheap way of asserting authority. But "to disparage [grammar] as empty formalism," as Sidney Harris wrote, is as foolish as, "venerating it as a sign of superiority." We've all found ourselves in disagreements that originated with a misunderstanding of something we said or wrote. Grammar in the broad sense of good communication would have prevented many of those unpleasantries. Who except the creative writer thinks ambiguity is "richness"?

The language ethic for most writers (and who isn't a writer these days?) should be clarity, economy, and precision. Attending to grammar is one of the best ways of achieving those results.

If artists are expected to learn to draw the human figure before dribbling paint on canvas, and musicians have to learn the scales before composing atonally, shouldn't writers have to master the fundamentals of grammar? As Hemingway said, "You ought to be able to show that you can write a good deal better than anyone else with the regular tools before you have a license to bring in your own improvements."

How long should your apprenticeship last? About 10,000 hours. That's how long it took before I could place a period after that fragment in good conscience.

Dear Dragonfly, Here Is Pepper Pod: Haiku Correspondence

"A piece of green pepper fell
off the wooden salad bowl:
so what?" —*Richard Brautigan*

"through the small holes
in the mailbox
sunlight on a blue stamp" —*Cor van den Heuvel*

Shortly after the Second World War, the Japanese Emperor sent an artful "letter" to his people. Though Hirohito had confessed himself a mortal, he still had an imponderable influence on his people, many of whom still worshipped him. At any rate, their ousted god wrote:

Under the weight of winter snow
The pine tree's branches bend
But do not break.

Some thought the royal haiku was a *wabi-sabi* expression of stoic calm, but the consensus in the Civil Censorship Detachment was that the verses were defiant. Nevertheless, perhaps in a conciliatory mood, the Americans allowed the "pebble-in-a-mossy-pond" poem to be published in newspapers across the country. Whatever the intent, as the pebble's circles spread, peace was restored, the occupation was lifted, the snow melted, and the pine branches proved resilient.

Over the last fifty years, I too have engaged in some haiku exchanges through the mail, over the telephone, in little magazines, and now by email. I have read of haiku

Twitter exchanges, but I've yet to tweet a twaiku.

My own exchanges began when I left an engineering curriculum at Georgia Tech in my freshman year, enlisted in the army, and met Dave Shuler a recent Oberlin College dropout. Dave was reading Harold Henderson's collection of haiku when I met him, and when he finished reading it, he gave it to me. It was the first book anyone outside my family had given me. Once we finished our military schooling, he was sent to Mt. Meissner, and I was sent to Heidwinkel/Bahrdorf, both in West Germany.

After reading Henderson's translations and plunging into the shallow form myself, I wrote Dave via the company's teletype on returning from field maneuvers:

Old stone fire pit—
The yellow flames sputter orange,
Blink, blue, and black out.

Dave replied more freely a few nights later:

Cool, gray, and smooth—
the airless flame
ablaze in flint.

The notion of cold fire lurking in flint was intriguing and remains so. Often when my shovel strikes a stone in the garden and a spark flares up, I think of Dave's haiku. And though I have lost touch with my friend, I hope he thinks of me when he loses himself in a chromatic analysis of fire.

After I was discharged, I returned to college as an English major and continued the alchemical struggle to turn seventeen syllables into gold. When Jane Morris, an old friend of the family, moved to Vermont to help care for her sick brother, I wrote her a haiku apropos of the season:

Does October's wind
throw sparks at heaven?
There's a burr in my sock.

After the first snow up north, Jane replied with a pungent memory of southern winters:

Carolina snow—
sweat runs down my back
and makes my sweater stink.

After an inexcusable pause, I wrote her back in the spring:

In my rain bucket,
skies and mayflies swim
in Appalachian snows.

When Jane's brother died that summer, she wrote:

Where's the daffodil
of yesteryear? A goldfinch
bobs up in the grass.

Advised by Jane that I would soon need an academic "union card," I returned to graduate school after reading the poetry of James Dickey, who was teaching at the University of South Carolina just two hours away. In the first of the classes I took from him, he instructed us to write five "breath poems" and gave us twenty unsigned examples including this one:

> A strange old man
> Stops me,
> Looking out of my deep mirror.

I still have the notes I took on that three-page handout, and while he never said he'd written the three lines I've quoted, he did say there were times he'd become a stranger to himself. Assuming he'd written the poem above, I wrote him the following:

> At the corners of the tent,
> the kids looked in,
> the clowns out.

Dickey was not amused, saying I'd written a senryu, another Japanese form which tends to be flippant and more topical than haiku. With eight typewriters in his home on eight desks for his eight latest poems, Dickey was a busy man.

When I resumed teaching, I would occasionally be invited to conduct a workshop in the local schools. Once after leading a group of sixth graders through the Clemson Forest looking for pine cones, wild strawberries, skulls, indeed, anything natural or seasonal which might trigger a haiku, a pink-cheeked girl I'll call "Jenny" submitted the following:

> Boys are very dumb.
> They make me puke all over.
> They throw snakes on you.

A pear-shaped admirer of Jenny's who wore a straw hat and chewed a stalk of grass wrote:

Jenny is sexy,
And she has a big behind,
But Jenny is fine.

This is not deathless haiku or even senryu, of course, but both "Jenny" verses were natural, and broadly interpreted, seasonal. Still, I was glad I did not have to grade them.

Naturally, the haiku written by my juniors and seniors at Clemson were more sophisticated. One student I'll call "Amy" told the workshop I was leading that her grandfather used to buy several watermelons at the farmers' market, bring them home in his pickup, and announce his return with a toot of his horn. As the visiting grandchildren ran to greet him, the grandfather would roll a melon off his tailgate under a shade tree. Amy wrote:

Split melon on the grass—
each seizes a slice
of the cool, dense heart.

Taken with this gustatory imagism, I replied with a melon haiku of my own:

the spoon turns
an egg—
the knife, wedges

Many years later, when our daughter, Anja, and family moved to Charlotte, North Carolina, they bought a long-in-the-tooth home in a gentrified neighborhood. After the first thunderstorm, Anja wrote:

> Lightning!
> And every nail in the house
> Gleams.

One of the house-warming gifts my wife and I had given Anja was a faceted crystal like the one she had enjoyed as a child chasing blurs of colored light around our kitchen. As grandparents, we wanted our grandchildren to enjoy the lights just as their mother had. Wrapped with this prism on a string, I added this:

> Sunlight strikes
> the beveled glass—
> rainbows!

In 1989, when my wife was recuperating from a mastectomy at Emory University Hospital, I wandered over to the library one afternoon while she napped. I'd seen a poster announcing the visit of some medieval "mercy seats" on loan from a cathedral in England. One showed a flock of chickens gleefully basting a spitted fox; another showed a pig playing a pigskin bagpipe, but my favorite was a worn carving of Eve before the Fall. I wrote several misericord senryu after that visit, and here's the last in the series:

> Centuries of monks
> have worn choirstall Eve
> flat chested.

In a fit of self-pity, I filed it away, for where would I send it?

In Billy Collins poem "Japan," he claims that reading a handful of haiku is like eating a bunch of grapes:

> ...the same small, perfect grape
> again and again.

But reading a hundred haiku submitted by twenty students new to the form is more like eating loose cherries from a paper bag: some sour, some over-ripe, and some perfect in taste and texture. Come to think of it, collections by definition are uneven.

So how does one find or write the perfect haiku? A decade ago, I culled everything I could lay my hands on for a workshop I was leading and compiled nineteen rules. But nineteen to an obsessive like me was a 5-7-4 haiku to Basho, so I added number twenty: "No good haiku follows all the rules." Indeed, I have read successful haiku that:

- rimed
- had two lines or four
- had more or fewer than seventeen syllables
- did not deal with a season
- discarded the pepper pods and kept the abstractions
- looked in more than out
- were allusive rather than illusive
- failed the balance of too much and too little
- gave us more of the slopes than the peak

So I've given up my attempts to define the form. There's more to be learned from the charcoal sketches of Michelangelo which have a completeness and perfection of their own. The master or his assistant kept a handful of his drawings and threw away the rest. Likewise, the haiku that evoke a smile, not laughter, and don't need a volume of commentary are the keepers. Now place those in an envelope and send them to someone you love.

Old Horses Do Not Die nor Do They Fade Away: Language Conservation

"Conservative means conserving—it implies preserving what is best and most valuable from the past, a decent respect for tradition, a reluctance to change merely for its own sake." —*Sidney J. Harris*

The US Army kept horse cavalry units until the end of WWII.
—*Various sources*

Republicans accustomed to clover worried that with the election of Barack Obama in 2007 the horses were gone, and the barn door was shut, but let me put their skittish minds at ease. The horse-and-buggy values of the Dubya era are as securely rooted as blue grass in Kentucky. Though horses started disappearing from America's roads and fields about a century ago, Pegasus is still kicking up his heels in English prose, poetry, and speech. Indeed, after studying the impact of horses on the language today, one might think they'd never gone to pasture. In a sense, they never did because most people reading this will understand it whether they think the Four Horsemen of the Apocalypse played for Notre Dame or Satan.

Let me illustrate the conservation of language whereby much is gained, but little is lost with some stories about my great grandfather Isaac "Hoss" Eisiminger born in 1857. Hoss operated a stable in Dobbin, Illinois from 1879 until his death in 1939, two years before I was born. A corn town of about three hundred, Dobbin never had a horsey set like Chicago. No one ever said, "Home, Hoss, and don't spare the horses" in his one-horse town. Whether you were full of oats or not, if you wanted to cross town, you took a horse with ten toes. Once before the turn of the century when Hoss took an iron horse to the alley-appled boulevards of Chicago, a maiden aunt with a little Latin but less French invited him for *hors d'oeuvres*. "But why," Hoss wondered, "would anyone make a meal of horse ovaries?"

As a boy, Hoss had been among those who mocked stranded motorists with, "Get a horse!" He'd been raised in an era when "adding horsepower" meant buying a third horse for the plow team. Of course, the horseless carriage eventually made its way to Dobbin, so Hoss, never one to depend on horseshoes nailed to the barn, changed horses in midstream. Unafraid of getting wet, Hoss believed that many business failures are caused by entrepreneurs reining in their horses prior to jumping. He was aided in this transition by his wife Ella, who urged him to "stop flogging a dead horse!" By 1925, better than half of his stable had been converted to a garage, and he owned a gas buggy himself. "If you can't ride two horses at once, you shouldn't be in the circus," said Hoss. In 1930, he sold "Bucephalus" and "Rosinante" to a Lincoln glue factory.

Small as Dobbin was, it fielded its own semi-pro baseball team, which played most summer Sundays before Prohibition in the state capital. The team, managed by Hoss, loved to horse around on the trip into the city, but they were a horse of a different color when it came to hitting and pitching the horsehide. The team recognized the truth of what Hoss preached, "Close only counts in barnyard golf." But whether the team won or wore a horse's collar, Hoss usually treated the boys to a horse opera at the Springfield Nickelodeon. If they didn't watch some flickering warhorse, they patronized a tavern near the stadium. Such a visit was less common because with some horse piddle in these farm boys the scene at the bar often turned into "horse apples and gun smoke," as Hoss liked to say.

I say "liked," but at home, Hoss knew "the gray mare was the better horse." Down at the stable, however, he sang a different tune for his mostly male clients: "If two must ride a horse, one must ride behind." Hoss's fondness for the stable led the family to joke, "I have to see a man about a horse" whenever they needed an excuse for just about anything.

Nevertheless, this blacksmith's family was well shod, and his children received good educations through the tenth grade, all that the local schools offered. Largely self-taught himself, Hoss knew the difference between horse sense and horse feathers (usage varied with the venue). To worsen matters, he'd seen too many young studs led to the academic waters of Champaign-Urbana without slaking their thirst.

In 1751, the first Eisimingers came to the New World seeking a haven from religious wars in Germany. Hoss's mother's Irish ancestors had fled similar conflicts in which thousands were killed or starved, so it was natural that this German-Irish-American was raised on stories of horse Protestant land owners dictating horseback opinions from their high horses. Despite the religious conflicts in the family, Hoss felt, "A man without religion is a horse without a bridle." Moreover, having grown up under the tutelage of horse traders on the jockey lots of central Illinois, Hoss was not going to back the wrong horse in the race of life. As far as he was concerned, God was not a dark horse, and wild horses were not going to change matters.

Never one to blame his saddle when he missed the mark, Hoss refused to don blinders as his life neared its close. Just as a good horse never goes straight up the hill,

Hoss knew the meandering way to the grave. The death of Ella in 1925 reinforced his belief that misfortune arrives on horseback but leaves on foot. When the mail brought a less-than-promised sum from his insurance company, Hoss looked that gift horse straight in the mouth. He'd read about the Greeks' parting gift to the Trojans, and he knew that one look inside might have saved a kingdom.

⁂

I began this essay by inviting Republican mavericks into the horse shed with the prospect of emerging as sidekicks.

In 2016, as the first African-American prepares to drop the reins of thermonuclear power, let me close by reminding my readers of Hoss's favorite axiom: "A good horse cannot be of a bad color."

Verbal Blindness: Illiteracy

Sixteen percent of the world's population or 775 million people cannot read.—*UN Human Development Report, 2013*

"The sword's in the book, not in the stone."—*The Wordspinner*

Alice, a friend, speaks no Spanish, but she recently hired Maria, a housekeeper, who speaks no English. Apparently, English-speaking housecleaners are beyond Alice's means. She bought, therefore, a Spanish-English dictionary, figuring that Post-It notes and a few penciled words would bridge the linguistic gap. Before Maria was scheduled to arrive one Saturday, Alice remembered that she wanted the living-room drapes washed, ironed, and rehung before she entertained that evening. But she had a morning bridge game and her husband had a golf tournament, so she took down the dusty drapes and laid them on the kitchen counter. Then she opened her dictionary and wrote: "*Por favor*: 1. *lavar*   2. *planchado*   3. *colgar. Gracias*," and laid the instructions on the drapes. It wasn't Cervantes, but she thought her three verbs would convey the gist of what she wanted. When she returned, however, she found Maria, who cannot read any language, in tears.

It should come as no surprise that Leo Tolstoy (1828-1910) had more readers in Europe than he had in Russia. The Russian serfs were not freed until 1861, and the educational system was slow to make amends. Compounding the problem, few illiterate serfs encouraged their children to read lest they leave home for Moscow or St. Petersburg. In this country, an estimated 10% of the slaves could read when they were emancipated in 1863, mainly because a handful of owners hoped their slaves would read the Bible. In fact, they did read the Bible as well as *Uncle Tom's Cabin* and reports of Nat Turner which fanned the embers of rebellion despite threats of whipping, amputation, and death. Unlike the runaway, the docile slave is often one who cannot read; Nat Turner probably read better than most who wanted him dead.

As I mentioned, 16% of the world's population is illiterate, and the UN report, where I culled that statistic, states that the US, like most of Europe, Russia, Australia, Japan, and Canada, is currently 99% literate. But what constitutes literacy is in dispute, for the National Assessment of Educational Progress found that 33% of US fourth graders in 2009 were illiterate, and 25% of US twelfth graders could not read at the lowest grade level. In 1996, a librarian in Tifton, Georgia, discovered that 92% of local elementary school students could not read a stop sign. In 2007, *Harper's* reported that one quarter of Americans had not read a book in the past year while 17% of British teens say they are embarrassed to be seen with a book. It bears repeating that the literate person who does not read or is embarrassed to read is little better off than one who cannot.

Though precise numbers are difficult to obtain, low literacy rates have been true for most of human history. As much as I'd like for there to be one, no culture has shown a perfect correlation between literacy and cultural longevity or economic success. Indeed, Sparta had no written laws because any Spartan who had to read them to know what they were "could not be trusted." Nevertheless, Sparta's golden era is just slightly longer than Athens', which venerated literacy.

No discussion of literacy would be complete without a nod to Charlemagne and his secretary of education, Alcuin. The enlightened but ruthless king probably could not write himself, but as a speaker of Old High German and Latin, he understood the importance of good communications as early as the eighth century. To that end, he financed the building of church schools and scriptoria throughout what became the Holy Roman Empire in 800. Within these schools, his edict of 787 ordered, "Take care to make no difference between the sons of serfs and freemen so that they may come to sit on the same bench to study grammar, music, and arithmetic." That we have anything of classical Greece and Rome to read is largely due to the writing centers that this German-Frankish king built or supported.

In these extraordinary places, he also supported the introduction of Carolingian minuscule, a clearer handwriting style than the crabbed Black Letter it replaced. And, though it seemed wasteful to many monks, he supported the practice of putting one space between letters, two between words, three between sentences, and indenting paragraphs. Some paleographers attribute the period, comma, question mark, and lower-case letters to the king who never mastered the proper grip of his golden stylus.

Nevertheless, by 1450, only 5% of adult males in Europe could read and write, and the numbers for women are even more discouraging. One of the ironies of the Enlightenment is that girls in many families were forbidden to take candles into the bedroom for fear that they might spend a few minutes reading. In 1850, before compulsory education began, the literacy rate in Massachusetts was 98%; since then, despite all efforts, it has never been higher than 91%.

But just as Frederick Douglass, a slave, and Malcolm

X, an inmate, taught themselves to read, so can most of us learn who are not in chains or prison. And while Ronald McNair, an astronaut, and Jesse Jackson, a minister, were denied books by their "public" libraries, so can the determined achieve some level of literacy. When my wife went to work in the business office of a university's food service, she noted that one fellow signed for his pay with an "X" and could not dial a telephone number without help. She worked with him over several weeks until he could sign his name and dial his home phone. It wasn't a Kenyan-kid-reading-in-the-moonlight sort of struggle; it's just that no one had ever bothered. After Sequoyah "bothered" to create his Cherokee syllabary, 95% of the tribe could read within five years of its introduction.

In 1943, my father was assigned a battalion of African-American draftees most of whom had failed to make the grade in artillery units. When it was apparent that their failure stemmed from their illiteracy, Dad and his officers adapted the Army's three-month Functional Literacy Program, or FLP, into a nine-week course in the three R's prior to the standard eleven-week course in combat engineering. The FLP and its variants are often credited with teaching a quarter-million GIs to read. His superiors rebuked him for the delay in getting his unit to the European theater, but Dad thought his men might bring the war to a swifter conclusion if they could read the labels on the pontoon bridges they would build and the explosives they would use to destroy canal locks. After the war, Dad said he was confident he'd lost no men in combat because they understood the orders and instructions they read while the Nazis had recruited men "who think with their thighs." Indeed, reading had enabled Dad to overcome the Mid-Western culture in which he was raised, namely, "Book larnin' ruins your shootin' eye." As if to refute that adage, one of Dad's men from Chicago shot down a Stork, a low-flying German reconnaissance plane with his carbine.

After I retired from teaching, I volunteered as a reading tutor at the local elementary school. "Jamaika" was assigned to me because she'd not been promoted to the third grade on the basis of her reading scores. We worked together for an entire school year—she'd read to me, or I'd read to her—and eventually, she recognized the commas and periods she'd once glided past. She also slowed down enough not to read phrases like "jumbled puzzle" as "jigsaw pizza" or some other "j- p-" combination that occurred to her. As her reading improved, however, she told me that her friends had started calling her "stuck-up" and accused her of "acting white." It's hard to protect anyone but especially a child when the people who should be her allies oppose her. By the second year, the modest gains "Jamaika" had made were sadly lost.

I recall hearing of a young woman who attributed her survival in a kayaking accident to balling up in a white-water hydraulic just as a character advised in Ron Rash's novel, *Saints at the River*. But life seldom works as smoothly as fiction. I think I recognized the limitations of reading and education in general when I read that Dietrich Bonhöffer and Otto Forbeck had been classmates and had thus read most of the same books. Bonhöffer matured to write the standard text on Lutheran *Ethics* and participate in a plot to assassinate Hitler. Forbeck matured to become a federal judge and a member of the Nazi SS. When Bonhöffer's plot failed, and he was arrested, Forbeck left a stranded train and rode a borrowed bicycle twenty kilometers in order to try and convict his former classmate.

For all of the shortcomings of education, we are

generally a better species when we can read freely. The best example of that today is South Korea, where less than half the population in 1945 could read. Seventy years later, 93% of its citizens are literate. Just across the northern border, the lights are usually out because the power supply is sporadic, but when the lights come on, there's little to read but propaganda.

※

In 2012, I read that Brazilian wardens were trying something novel: for every approved book that inmates read and wrote a report on, officials have agreed to reduce sentences by four days per book. Lest speed readers get out of jail too soon, the reduction is limited to forty-eight days a year. If full advantage is taken, a four-year sentence is reduced to 3.5 years, and inmates leave prison with forty-eight books in their heads. Though some will surely abuse the privilege, it sounds like a clever way to ease tensions in crowded jails, cut unemployment, and fill municipal coffers.

Multiplying One by Two: Imitation

"Imitation is suicide." —*Ralph Waldo Emerson*

"Go, and do thou likewise." —*Luke 10:37*

The earliest extant examples of two and three-dimensional art were meticulous copies drawn from life. The more realistic the bison painted on the cave walls of Lascaux in 30,000 BC, the more bison spirit was tamed, and the greater the probability of a successful hunt, or so they may have believed. About the same time, the more realistic the carvings of pregnant women, the greater the probability that real women would reproduce, or so they may have believed.

Often, however, life imitates art. I don't know of a better illustration of this point than Morgan Robertson's novel *Futility* published in 1898, fourteen years before the *Titanic* sank. In the novel, an ocean liner attempting to cross the North Atlantic from the UK to the US in record time smashes into an iceberg, drowning most on board. The name of this fictitious ship is the *Titan*. Moreover, like its doomed sister, the *Titan* sinks in April, has three screws to drive it at a similar top speed, is about 800' long with a similar displacement tonnage, carries too few lifeboats for about the same number of passengers, and is advertised as "unsinkable." Now, imagine Mr. Robertson's face when he read of reality stealing his plot. To his credit, he never tried to capitalize on this remarkable series of coincidences.

But sometimes life just imitates life. There is, for example, a beetle that has learned to imitate the mating code of a female firefly. Thus, an aroused male, blinded by his passion, may find himself in the maw of his "lover."

Finally, there's the long tradition of art imitating art. For all we know, the "Woman of Willendorf," alluded to above, may have been a copy of an older fertility fetish, but generally, the newer the work, the more certain historians can be of the derivation. Take the Basilica of Our Lady of Peace which was "personally financed" by President Félix Houphouët-Boigny at a cost of $300,000,000. This Roman Catholic structure on the plains of the Ivory Coast is so large that St. Peter's Basilica, once the world's largest church, would fit inside. But grandeur was not "Papa" Houphouët's only aim. He was so intent on verisimilitude that he imported thirty acres of marble from the same quarries Michelangelo had used. Moreover, he was so determined that his people would remember his magnanimity, he had himself enshrined kneeling before Jesus in one of the basilica's largest windows. In 1989, the doors were opened to worshippers in a country that is predominately Muslim.

Works such as this pile in the bush are a form of self-colonization. On a smaller, personal scale, the basilica reminds me of Peter Singh who once performed songs like "My Poppadum Told Me" under the stage name, "the Pakistani Elvis." Thanks to his American mentor, who occasionally appears to him in a dream, Singh claims he has stopped drinking alcohol and smoking marijuana.

Indeed, casting the same shadow as one you admire can be a rewarding exercise. The problem for acolytes like Mr. Singh is that there are an estimated 85,000 Elvis impersonators across the globe, twenty-eight in Vegas alone. In an era when over a hundred adults are making a living impersonating Marilyn Monroe, and Charlie Chaplin can do no better than fourth place in a "Charlie Chaplin Look Alike Contest," and Graham Greene has to settle for second place in a "Graham Greene Parody Contest," there's something wrong with imitation as a lifelong philosophic formula. As Cary Grant, born Archibald Leach, said, "Everybody wants to be Cary Grant. Even I want to be Cary Grant."

In the 1970s, every male swimmer wanted to be Mark Spitz. In the 1972 Olympics, Spitz had won seven gold medals breaking seven world records in the process. After the games, a Russian coach asked the American swimmer if his famed mustache didn't slow him down. "No," replied Spitz with a smile, "as a matter of fact, it deflects water away from my mouth [which] allows my rear end to rise...." The following year, most male Russian swimmers sported a mustache in international competition.

As with most paradigms, there are extremes which call the middle into question. Examples of the imitation paradigm gone appallingly wrong include nearly three hundred copies of the Tylenol poisonings and twenty-six suicides following *The Deer Hunter*. On the good side, there's the case of 115 British soldiers surrendering in the American Revolution when they were fooled by a "Quaker cannon," a hollow log painted to look like gun metal and mounted on a carriage.

At this point, you may be asking, "Is cubic zirconia the equivalent of a diamond?" Yes and no, I would equivocate. Would you object if I told you that in "Curse of the Pink Panther," David Niven's last film, his voice was dubbed by Rich Little, the comic impersonator? Niven was deathly ill and unavailable for any retakes, but to me the film is still a gem.

Benjamin DeMott argued that the literature teacher's foremost duty is to "harry imaginations into constructing the innerness of other lives." I have long thought that going to the theater, the ballet, the opera, the movies, or reading fiction is the best way for humans to learn empathy. I think that because by identifying with everyone from Mother Goose to Huck Finn I learned empathy, and no amount of reading undramatized philosophy or theology has convinced me otherwise.

The risk, of course, lies in fixating on a mentor, theory, or style and never developing the uniqueness that is every human's birthright. I've read that traditional Indian singers drone behind their masters for years. At some point, the apprenticeship ends, and the protégé comes to the fore. I would wish that for each of us.

Visiting museums, I often like to take a seat behind a young artist copying an Old Master. I pretend to be studying the Vermeer or the Rubens on the wall, but I'm really trying to get a sense of whether this apprentice to the dead is developing or just copying the dusty work in the gilded frame. She alone is she, for that is nature's gift, but it's left to each to establish a brand.

Booing in the Free Seats: Ingratitude

"Those with free seats are the first to hiss." —*Chinese proverb*

"Ask for nothing and give thanks for what's yours.
Then, hark to the heather that speaks on the moors."—*The Wordspinner*

I'll never forget reading one student's free-write journal—fifty pages of implacable woe concluding with what surely was a cry for help. "Mary," I'll call her, had gained twenty pounds by her second semester; her live-in boyfriend was threatening to leave; she had no friends; she could not stop smoking or fall asleep; she hated her neighbors, her hair, her nails, her complexion, and her church; she was failing two courses and had entertained thoughts of suicide in high school. Yet, all of this was well written with a few touches of self-deprecating humor and the occasional allusion to Ophelia. She had a strong "B" in my class where she was usually well prepared and unafraid to start a discussion.

An illness she'd contracted over Easter, however, caused her to miss a grammar quiz, so when she returned to school, she came by the office to make it up and retrieve her journal. When she'd finished the quiz, I tried to draw her out, but she was not in a conversational mood. I left the office myself a short while later, and as I was waiting for the elevator, I glanced in the trash where her "A+" journal lay. I fished it out and re-read my final comment: "Do yourself a favor, Mary, and keep this going—you have a real flair for the confessional, which is often good therapy. Come by any time if you'd like to talk."

I felt something like the protagonist in John Steinbeck's

story "The Chrysanthemums" who'd given a handsome but manipulative tinker some flower bulbs she was transplanting only to find them later scattered across the highway to town. But reality is frequently more disappointing and certainly more personal than fiction. I'm thinking of a dying friend who told his all-American son-in-law, "I'm leaving you my Honda." Said the son-in-law, "Thanks, but I don't drive foreign cars." But worse was a friend of our son who lent his tennis partner $200 to help pay his rent. A short while later, the two were invited to an out-of-town tournament. After they'd checked into their motel room, and while the lender was fetching some ice, the debtor stole $200 from his partner's wallet. He later "repaid" his debt with an unctuous, "I don't know how to thank you!"

At the core of "gratitude" is a root meaning "favor." I find this interesting because we know the Indo-Europeans and their Germanic descendants kept a record of favors, indicating as it did one's social station. As the language shows, favors could be bestowed, obtained, or lost: a "gratuity" was a material favor; to "congratulate" was to bestow an oral favor; to be "disgraced" was to fall from favor; an "ingrate" had no favor, to "ingratiate" was to worm oneself into another's favor, and "grace" was a sign of God's favor.

Along similar linguistic lines, the Old High German for "thanks" (*danken*) is related to "think" (*denken*) because the ancients intuitively understood that there is no true gratitude without thought *and* feeling. Indeed, both senses are present in "thank." In other words, a thank-you shouldn't be thoughtless. One Christmas, my wife baked several loaves of banana bread and took one to our financial advisor, who, Ingrid learned from the receptionist, was hospitalized. Slipping into the advisor's office unannounced, she placed the gift with its bright red bow on the assistant's desk and said, "Merry Christmas!" Though he had a mountain of paperwork about him, he sprang to his feet, went to a storage closet, returned with a can of Febreze, and handed it to Ingrid. Perhaps he was benighted by his work, but "Thanks," is all he said.

We have a right to expect gratitude from family and friends, but the people we work for have an obligation as well. Yet the New York Transit Authority and 7-Eleven administrators warn employees about the limits of executive gratitude. In 1994, one New York bus driver was docked a day's pay after pulling a man from a burning car and clocking in twelve minutes late. In 2000, a 7-Eleven employee was fired when he wrestled the gun away from a thief and chased him from the premises. Though the manager prevented a robbery, he was fired for violating company policy. Harsh, I say: I would have sent both men to a safety counselor then given them a bonus.

I remember explaining to some sophomore students of Greek literature why looking a gift horse in the mouth would be considered rude. When I finished, one young man wondered how a war we'd recently read about might have been affected if the Trojans had examined that big hollow horse left at their gate. When I recovered, I said perhaps we should say, "Don't look a gift horse in the mouth—unless it comes from your enemy." Indeed, gift horses like white elephants have always been a trial. Thus, if you receive one, give private thanks to the donor and the gods. You might want to build a barn and take out some insurance as well.

Nature gives everyone a gift horse—namely, the bad things that happen to others. If there were no gods, as Voltaire said, we'd have to invent them just to give thanks.

✳

In the 1960s, when my wife and I were living in Columbus, Georgia, my uncle Ted owned a motel in Panama City, Florida. After a meal Ingrid prepared for him, he invited us to come down to the Beachcomber whenever we wanted. Over a five-year period, I believe we took him up on the offer three or four times. We always called before coming; we always cleaned up after ourselves; we always thanked him personally after a visit, and, indeed, as far as we were aware, we never abused our privilege. At the time, we could not afford to go to the beach unless we went on my uncle's dime, so we were admittedly featherbedding the golden goose.

One Fourth of July, Ted's maids declared their independence when my sometimes unpredictable uncle asked them to ride ten miles to work on the back of a truck. To help out, my wife and I answered the office phone, swept sand from the sidewalks, and changed some soiled sheets. The following summer, Ted and I found ourselves sitting on the motel's patio sharing a beer and watching the sun set. Suddenly, he turned to me and said, "Skip, you have to stop being so ungrateful." Of course I wanted an explanation, but his office manager yelled that he had a phone call, and we left early the next morning. A few weeks later, we moved out of state. Though I asked for details more than once, several years later, he died without ever explaining. In a courtroom, I would have had a chance to cross-examine, but since I was denied that, I'll just say, "Thank you, Uncle Ted. I'm sorry for my ingratitude, but it was unintentional."

Ted's father used to say you can't put milk back in the cow, but if there's a spill, the cleanup is easier if you know where it is.

Called Home by the Divine Afflatus: Inspiration

"Dust is the stuff on which vapor condenses—
out of the wind, a poem commences." —*The Wordspinner*

"The poet must hold each black-or-white face
even while musing the black-or-white vase." —*The Wordspinner*

I was drawn to write my MA thesis on the poet Randall Jarrell in part because of his calculated candor. "A poet," he wrote, "spends a lifetime in a thunderstorm and is lucky to be hit by lightning five or six times." In my mid-twenties, I was still waiting for the rain. A few years later, the poet James Dickey told a class, "A poet is someone who stands outside in the rain hoping to be struck by lightning." At that time, it was just drizzling, but it seemed to me that Jarrell and Dickey had pointed their lightning rods at the *Zeitgeist* and drawn out the truth electric: namely, the muse is quicksilver. I'm still waiting for the lightning, but when a bee crawls under my bonnet, I'm happy to take a few stings for the sake of Art.

Struggling with a piece of writing, I sometimes think that Shakespeare and Milton drew the muse's batteries so low she's still recharging. Given the unprecedented number of artists standing in the rain imploring the heavens, it's no wonder inspiration has been spread so thin in recent years. In recognition of the number of poets and the dearth of good poetry, Robert Graves thought poets should be given twenty small silver plates on which to engrave their life's work. But the volatile muse has never been an egalitarian, which is probably wise, or I'd be as good as Shakespeare, or Shakespeare would be as good as Eisiminger, depending on whether she leveled up or down.

Of all the ways artists have courted the muse, the technique of British romantic Llewelyn Powys is perhaps the most eccentric. Powys concluded that Erato and her sisters would be drawn to anyone who washed their underclothes "with their own hands," kept "as far as possible from animals foods," slept "with the windows wide open," and caught "a glimpse of the sea *every morning*." (Powys's italics) I do an occasional load of laundry, and I do like to sleep with the windows open in the spring, but living, as my wife and I do, some two hundred miles from the sea perhaps explains why I'm still waiting for the lightning.

As an erstwhile academic poet, I've long been enrolled in W. H. Auden's "College for Bards." His curriculum requires a lifelong study of one ancient and two modern languages in addition to English. I haven't studied Latin or French in many years, but my German wife helps to keep my *Deutsch* current even though the bees in my bonnet usually buzz in English. Auden also recommends cultivating a garden, keeping a pet, taking electives in meteorology and cooking, memorizing poetry, and writing parodies. Though Auden was a fine critic himself, books of criticism are banned from his library. I doubt that Shakespeare and Milton read much criticism because there wasn't much of it, but many of the prosaic insights of Jarrell and Dickey are inspired.

In one class, Dickey said that if poets wanted "the juice," it would behoove them to write narratives because "everyone wants to know what happens next." That simple but true observation in itself was worth reams of critical bombinating in a theoretical void. Indeed, Dickey's poem "The Shark's Parlor" and Jarrell's "The Death of the Ball Turret Gunner" have gripping stories to tell.

Regardless of where the inspiration comes from or how

it's expressed, there's always the "anxiety of influence" to cope with, especially when young. One of the best teachers and smartest people I've ever had the pleasure to know, Auburn's Dr. Carl Benson, told a class once that after he read Yeats's poetry, he gave up all hope of ever writing another poem. How sad and unnecessary.

It took me years to overcome that same anxiety and accept whatever the muse gave me. But basically, I just repressed the fear and placed my shoulder against a muddy wheel while Pegasus was grazing. A sympathetic spouse, a productive routine, long slow bike rides, and a desire to leave something for our children sustained me. Yeats had some wonderful experiences to draw on; but once I realized my own experiences were interesting to family, friends, and students, I was released from the shackles of influence. If I were a young pianist, however, and I saw a video of twelve-year-old Grammy nominee Joey Alexander, I'd probably burn the piano.

One way I discovered to "precipitate" the muse is by creating a "supersaturated solution." For years I have collected smart quotations, photographs, cartoons, personal anecdotes, interesting statistics, etc. and pasted these on 3x5 cards. When I sense the presence of the muse, I steep myself in forty years' worth of material washed by all waters. It's a form of brainstorming or induced serendipity, but no one else is actively involved. The essay before you was released from its "suspension" by first mixing two dozen "ingredients."

As Emerson, another "ingredient," writes in "The American Scholar," the muse is not going to give instructions on how or what to write, but she will provide the need to write, or as Emerson wrote, the provocation. Musicians have told me that she often provides a haunting tune, but the development and orchestration are left to the composer.

Scientists often depend on visual analogues for inspiration such as the wasp nest that led to paper made of wood pulp. Artists, on the other hand, are often stimulated less directly via the nose, tongue, skin, and ears. Samuel Johnson needed orange peels and a cup of tea on his desk. Schiller famously needed the smell of rotting apples. As he was going deaf, Beethoven dowsed himself with cold water to resuscitate the music dying in his head. Dickens found it difficult to write unless he'd slept in a bed aligned with the North Pole. Proust needed a sound-proof room, but Mark Strand needed a loud television. And Fran Lebowitz just needs a cab to drive her around New York City.

⌘

Sometimes the muse holds a gun to your head; other times, she sits on your shoulder and insists you need another beer. And sometimes Abuse, a stepsister, comes uninvited, looks over your shoulder, and whispers, "What rubbish!" Even so, it's best to keep your lightning rod polished.

Will Rogers Never Met My Aunt: Insults

"What he lacked in size he made up for in speed." —*Anonymous ex-wife*

"Cross the river before insulting the crocodiles." —*Confucius*

I've heard that if gloves aren't available you should dig your fingernails into a bar of soap before wielding a tar brush because insults have a way of lodging under the nails. I was in an Emeritus College meeting recently when a friend said that he'd retired while he "was still young and beautiful." A recent retiree I had not met before said, "Does that mean you're old and ugly now?" Said my friend picking up the tar brush, "Welcome to the club."

Knowing when to shut up is something I thought I'd learned years ago. Evidently, I haven't. In an abnormally quiet spin class, I asked our thirty-something instructor if she'd heard that Ben, a regular member of the class, had finished third in the Charlotte Triathlon.

"That's terrific," she replied. "What age group did he compete in?

"I'd guess twenty-five to thirty."

"No way," she said, "Ben can't be more than twenty-two." And with that she hopped off her bike and went to check at the front desk. A short while later, she returned and said, "You're right—he's twenty-six." I smiled and said it was a gift. An attractive woman spinning beside me said, "So, how old do you think I am?" I sensed a trap, but I'd seen her in cycling shorts and T-shirt enough times that I was pretty sure she was in her early thirties. Hence, I decided to pay her a compliment and said, "Twenty-nine."

"The hell you say, mind reader—I'm not twenty-four yet."

I fumbled an apology and offered her a chance to get even: "How old do you think I am?"

"Sixty-two," she said low-balling her answer.

"I'm seventy, but thank you all the same." As we were walking to our cars, I repeated my apology, but I knew she'd never forgive me. "Ageless, you idiot," I said to myself. "Why didn't you tell her she's ageless?"

My grandfather used to say that "if you're throwing dirt, you're losing ground," but his daughter took her own counsel. Aunt Julie had no qualms insulting anyone, but her "cod liver oil" was always delivered in "a sugar tit." She told me once, "Skipper, your mother's talents [as a painter] lie south of the wrist—bless her heart." That phrasal suffix is a time-worn strategy that arose with the South when it was still occupied by northern troops, and it tastes like green strawberries drizzled in chocolate.

For all her offensive skills, however, Julie never mastered the defensive art of what I call "resemblance" and others name the "marshmallow apologia." Imagine my aunt telling the Italian tenor Guido Nazzo, "Guido, honey, your performance tonight was Nazzo Guido." Now Guido of Newark will surely resent that crack, but the proper retort would be, "I resemble that remark." The comic malaprop immediately dresses the wound and gives Julie a chance to poke around in her purse and proffer a bandage.

In a similar vein, a straight-faced woman once told TV's Dr. Frazier Crane, her ex-boyfriend, that when she compulsively had sex with him a year ago, she'd "hit bottom," but, she added, "that was a prerequisite to my rebounding." To his credit, the often put-upon shrink quietly said, "I'm glad I was down there for you." Had he whined about how sub-memorable she was, he might have exposed himself as a mate for the ingrate she revealed herself to be.

The language maven David Grambs once set up two columns of twenty-nine words each that one could select from when framing a modifier-noun insult. "King-sized peabrain," he suggested, is a contradiction. "Royal nitwit" is clichéd. And "stupid numskull" is as redundant as "real baboon" is prolix. Yet if one considers the smoldering Arab garbage collector in Tel Aviv, one soon realizes that insults are useful at times especially when muttered under one's breath behind enemy lines. Drawing from the same lists that produced the four duds above, one might create the alliterative "drooling dipstick" or the obscure "egregious stoopnagel." What's more effective than calling out one's enemy and sending him to the dictionary to discover his punishment?

Since I alluded to the Jews, who mastered the veiled and unveiled insult during the Diaspora, let me remind you of Colette Avital. In 2001, this Israeli lawmaker published a list of words and phrases that she wished to ban from parliamentary debate. Had her proposal passed, legislators would no longer be able to use "filth," "hypocrite," "pig," "Nazi," "nincompoop," and a score of others in the halls of the Knesset. But as much as I hate to admit it, there are Nazi swine among us, and often one needs to call a club a club. I'll leave the spade in the garden shed.

With an abundance of nincompoops in these parts, white Southerners have been honing their vilifications since Reconstruction. The "Caucasian dozens," as I call them, allow us to call Mr. Potato Head and turkeys like him "a spud." The dialectal options also include: "His dough ain't done," "He ain't wrapped real tight," and, "He's a full bubble off plumb." For the religiously inclined, we have, "He wasn't bitten by Solomon's dog." As the baker's dozens moved north, mathematically inclined Yankees have added a numerical component: "He's one tree shy of a hammock," or, "She's three floats shy of a parade." In Minnesota, Garrison Keillor reports that there are some Norwegian bachelors who are "all wax and no wick." Over in Texas, they say, "Manuel's one taco shy of a combo platter." And in San Francisco, my sister tells me, they say, "The brie slid off Bruce's cracker long ago."

I mention my sister because a few years ago she sent me a Billy Graham column in which he wrote, "Judgment's the dark line in the face of God." I wrote her back saying I believed half of what Graham was saying, but from where I sit, I cannot tell if that dark line is a frown or a smile. It's just that my sister's Calvinistic faith encourages her to insult others with threats of hellfire when there can never be any determination the living are aware of. For myself, I'll shut my mouth and assume the best until I know otherwise.

Chalking the Slate: Learning

"I want young people to grow up so that they will frighten the world, a violent, dominant, cruel youth....I do not want intellectual education." —*Adolf Hitler*

"[Henry Burlingame, the tutor] taught [the twins] to wonder at a leaf of thyme, a line of Palestrina, the configuration of Cassiopeia, the scales of a pilchard, the sound of 'indefatigable,' the elegance of sorites. The result of this education was that they grew quite enamored of the world." —*John Barth*

British dairies began making home deliveries in 1920. The following year, a blue tit was observed in Swaythling, a village southwest of London, prying off a milk bottle's cardboard cap and drinking the cream. By the 1930s, the birds were observed prying off caps throughout the London and Midlands area. By the early 1940s, the practice had spread to Ireland, and by 1950, it had spread to Scotland. Whether "Newton," as he came to be called, offered seminars in cap removal or simply allowed his young to observe him is not known, but clearly the skill was disseminated.

Some species, however, are more gifted than others in knowledge acquisition and transference. One wasp species depends on grasshoppers to provide the ideal meal plan for their larvae. Once a hopper has been stung to death, the wasp pulls the insect by its antennae to its burrow. However, if the antennae have been removed in the struggle, the wasp has no idea how to grasp another appendage and thus has no place to lay its eggs. This is why nature allows the brains of larger, more complex animals to acquire knowledge on their own, freeing them from the shackles of instinct.

When a human fetus is cut free of its umbilical, it

possesses several unlearned reflexes like nursing, heartbeat, respiration, and excretion, but that does not mean the slate is blank. Indeed, our slates are thoroughly scribbled upon at birth. Babies are born crying with their mothers' accent; they prefer the same foods their mothers have been eating over the last three months; they can hold their breath and "swim," and they recognize not only their mothers' voices, but the theme songs of their favorite soap operas.

Like a bird flapping its wings and hopping in the nest practicing take-offs and landings, humans start beating their wings for the truth from the start, but learning takes place on a continuum. In April of 2008, I volunteered to drive our four-year-old granddaughter and her twelve-year-old brother to school one morning. On the way, Lena said she was looking forward to "show and tell." I naturally asked her what she was going to share, and she said, "The moon."

"What *is* the moon?" I wondered aloud.

"It's a circle," she replied.

"No, it isn't," her brother replied. "It's a ball."

"Actually, Spencer," I said, "the moon is like the earth—an irregular oblate ellipsoid. And one day, we may describe it as something else again." You can imagine the frowns I glimpsed in my mirror.

But learning produces frowns at any point on the continuum especially at an advanced age. Once, a sixty-something woman showed up at a spin class I was part of. She said her doctor had recommended stationary cycling for her heart. The class welcomed her, and the instructor helped her adjust her seat and handlebars. How to pedal was assumed to be part of her schooling, but in fact she didn't know. She'd never ridden a bicycle before. Try as she might, she pulled her feet out of the traps designed to keep the balls of the feet centered on the pedals. "Push down on the balls of your feet, and then pull up with the top of your foot," the instructor told her, but it was no use: she kept pulling her feet back and off the pedals. She was so embarrassed she left and has not returned.

I know how she felt. I tried to learn some line-dance steps in a Zumba class a few years ago and failed miserably. I *might* have learned, but I was in a class with several younger people, and they caught on much quicker than I did. Though no one was laughing at me, I gave up like the spinner after convincing myself that I didn't need line dancing on my résumé. Nor did I need to finish *Moby Dick*, but I do respect the never-say-die spirit of those who have harpooned that beast of a book.

I recall a photograph of a boy I consider the ideal student—not just a willing student but a passionate one. The boy had been blinded in an explosion which also took his hands and feet, but his disabilities did not leave him helpless. Indeed, his determination to learn Howard Nemerov's "Three dozen bits and pieces of a stuff / So arbitrary, so peremptory, / That worlds invisible and visible / Bow down before it...." was palpable even in two dimensions. He'd taught himself to read braille pressing his lips and nose to the textured pages.

Larry Abernathy, an old friend, colleague, and teammate, grew up with a different set of disabilities. As Larry often acknowledged, he was raised homophobic, racist, and sexist, but over the six years it took to acquire three degrees in this university town of ours, he learned the error of his ways. Ludwig Wittgenstein said, "The limits of my language mean the limits of my world." When Larry enrolled at Clemson, he came with a limited "vocabulary," but he acquired one by investing the requisite "10,000 hours." He read himself clear of his past. When he died after twenty-eight years as mayor of Clemson, he was mourned by gays and straights, blacks and whites, men and women.

I thought of the blind boy mentioned above as I walked into our municipal library one summer Saturday. In the children's section were a dozen or so Asians and Indians waiting for "Story Hour." You should know that black and white children live within walking and biking distance of the library, and for those who don't, the city provides free bus service. Sadly, many of the children who most need the stimulus were not present, and according to one librarian, this attendance pattern is typical.

I hope the non-Asian children were home reading a book or tinkering with a lawnmower, but anti-intellectualism is not the greatest obstacle to learning. It's the certainty of the knowledge we already have. In Clyde Edgerton's novel *Raney*, a fundamentalist wife tells her back-sliding husband, "The Bible warns against lusting in your heart. That's all I need to know about the subject. That's all I'm supposed to know about the subject. That's all I want to know about the subject. That's all there *is* to know about the subject." All of which opposes the wisdom of Hosea who states, "People are destroyed for lack of knowledge."

Like Raney, many married to the church are mired somewhere east of Eden with an attitude that pits them against my own educational philosophy:

"Look hard to see the sand in the pearl;
teach students to love all of the world."

Whether my blind hero, who's seen "the sand in the pearl," is a fox or a hedgehog, he understands that his teachers are not talking heads. Before, during, and after class, he interacts with them if necessary and his texts because he realizes he is as responsible for his education as his parents and teachers. I imagine that before my hero set sail, he fell in love with one word, or book, or writer, or subject, and he built on that, for as he's surely learned, love is a better teacher than authority.

The Truth About Some Lies: Fibbing

"To use speech, then, for the purpose of deception … is a sin." — *St. Augustine*

"Lying is acceptable if peace demands it." —*Rabbi Ille'a*

Had St. Augustine, Immanuel Kant, or John Wesley opened Otto Frank's door in 1944 and been asked by an SS officer if Anne and her family were home, all three presumably would have answered, "Why yes, sir, they live in the attic." On the other hand, had Rabbi Ille'a, author of my second epigraph, been asked the same question, I imagine he would have replied, "I'm sorry, sir, but there's no one here but me, Heinrich von Hindenburg."

I can wait, but I'm looking forward to learning which of those four including the Roman Catholic saint made it to heaven. One scholar actually tried to excuse Kant by having him say nothing to the Nazi officer in the clichéd scenario, but that to me is the same as pointing to the door hidden by the bookshelves. Pressured innocence is rarely silent, and Hitler's agents surely knew that.

We lie by some estimates fifteen to thirty times a week, minimizing in one breath and exaggerating in the next. These numbers should come as no surprise given the half-truths our pop culture is rife with. Much advertising, for example, consists of a tissue of misrepresentations that have entered the language as catch phrases, including: "Your refund is in the mail"; "Limited time offer"; "If X [an eighteen-year-old gymnast] can lose weight, you can too"; "Actual mileage may vary," and my favorite, "Easy to install."

We lie to spare our friends' feelings and to keep secrets that we know will cause needless suffering if revealed. Indeed, our dictionaries are bursting with the ways we dodge, warp, stretch, and twist the truth. We are two-faced and double-dealing as we put people on and perjure ourselves. We run with the hares and hunt with the hounds; we shoot the shit, bullshit, and misspeak. We garble, gloss, and paper over; fudge, embroider, and deodorize; cook the numbers and juggle the books; salt a mine and speak with a forked tongue. We draw the long bow, go through the motions, and put on a false front. We sail under false colors and work both sides of the street; indeed, we will say almost anything to avoid using "lie" as a verb with "I" as its subject.

Nevertheless, I am here to champion half-truths and white lies, those fibs and falsehoods that level the playing field. I've long admired that last metaphor which, I suspect, is used too often without reflection. I used to tell Clemson students to imagine playing the Gamecocks on a slanted field where the 'Cocks are defending from the high ground and running downhill on offense. It just isn't fair play.

When a rapist holds a knife at a woman's throat, there is *nothing* ethically wrong if she says, "I must warn you—I've tested positive for the HIV virus—I have AIDS." The woman's lie simply evens the odds by giving her a verbal knife which she holds at her assaulter's groin. The trust that is society's fabric is in no way threatened. Yes, the assaulted has told a lie; she has borne false witness, but is there a jury in the world that would convict her? Is any fabric torn but her blouse?

I recall reading about the Columbine High massacre in which one of the two shooters entered the school cafeteria where several students hid trembling under the tables. As one of the psychopaths moved from table to table kicking aside the chairs, he asked, "Do you believe in God?" If the answer was affirmative, the student was shot, and the shooter moved on.

After thinking about that scenario, I asked some Clemson sophomores if they would have denied God to avoid death in a similar situation. Not one said they would. "I'm sorry," as I told them, "but personally, I would have said anything to take that weapon out of the shooter's hand. I have no respect for a god who is going to ship me to hell for denying him when there's a gun at my head." I told the class they were welcome to their beliefs, but in my view of heaven, those Jews who became "Lutherans" to avoid going to Auschwitz are seated alongside their maker. Whether the anti-Semitic Martin Luther is there is another matter.

A few days later in the same semester, I led a discussion of Arthur Miller's historical parable *The Crucible*. In the closing scenes, a reformed Rev. Hale begs Goody Proctor to encourage her husband, John, to make a false confession, for that alone might save him from the gallows. The class wondered whether it was wise to discuss this strategy within earshot of the colony's governor and the Salem judge, who brooked no denials of witchcraft. But the law did spare the lives of the accused if they confessed their crime. Unfortunately, that did not prevent the state from confiscating all their material possessions and turning families out of their homes.

"Cleave to no faith when faith brings [death]," Rev. Hale advises Elizabeth. "I beg you … let him give his lie." This time, most of the students agreed that perjury would have been "a courageous sin." Tragically, Elizabeth was unsuccessful, for John opted to protect what remained of his reputation. He was executed with nineteen of his neighbors and two dogs.

In *The End of Faith*, Sam Harris tells a fascinating story of how he prevented a kidnapping with the only weapon he had, his voice. In a Prague alley, he came upon several drunks trying to force a woman into a car. Courageously, Harris approached the thugs, and in what I consider a stroke of genius, he began mangling his English to divert the Czech abductors. "No! Not *sex*," he exclaimed, "I am looking for a specific building. It has no aluminum siding or stained glass. It could be filled with marzipan. Do you know where it is?" Caught off guard by this dizzying diversion, the captors released their grip on the woman who then slipped away.

Astonishingly, however, Harris said he came to consider his "lies" a "moral failure" because he had "made no effort to communicate" to the men, who "never received any correction from the world." Sam, Sam, Sam—you could have run away and left the victim to be raped or killed. If I ever face a similar dilemma, I hope I remember your gibberish tactic because it may produce the fair shake I'm endorsing.

When the mother of a friend decided she'd had all she could take from her son's pet goat, who was killing all the fruit trees in the family's back-yard orchard, she gave the animal to her brother who lived on a farm out of town. My friend Harold, who was six at the time, was assured that out in the country the goat would have room to play and plenty of friends. A few months later, mother and son went to visit the goat. "Where's Smelly?" Harold asked.

"We et him," the uncle replied.

Not, "We gave him to a traveling circus"; just, "we et him."

A lie would have been ever more generous.

Musings of an Affectionado: Malapropisms I and II

"Simply put, a malapropism is impropaganda." —*The Wordspinner*

"Quilting is a useful hobby for the elderly, wherein the crap of a lifetime can be turned into a patchwork comforter." —*The Wordspinner*

I.

With deciduous application, Ilse had kept the dark horses of evil at bay during the Nazi error. However, nuclear weapons terrified her, so she placed all her eggs in one basket case, namely herself, dodged a fuselage of bullets crossing the Check border, and fled to Civil, Spain. But when she heard John Lenin singing "Imagine" on the radio, she tied up all her dead ends and fled once more. "Fortunately," she was heard to say, "I am affluent in English, so New Pork is the obvious choice." Before leaving Spain, however, she called a tax attorney to stuff her dog.

Arriving in New Pork, Ilse shouted, "Terra firma at last!" but she had merely cracked pandemonium's box. "Funny how the best intentions go a rye," she later mused. Determined, nevertheless, to make a go of it, she towed the line and exorcised daily. Though she lived in a chantey by the tracks, she hired a tooter, who helped her make progress toward a white-color job: lab assistant for the Autobahn Society. "I've always been good at mounting," she told the interviewer.

It was in this capacity that Ilse met Max, a circus-sized country pumpkin with a vast suppository of knowledge. Innocently, she had stopped her Honda Hunchback to ask directions when he appeared. She almost left when he admitted he was on the lamb, but when he promised her multiple organisms, she couldn't resist. As for Max, he couldn't take his eyes off Ilse's decoupage and dairy air. Long a woman of mammary distinction, Ilse thought, "Now here's a man I can neuter." They started drinking hopscotch on the rocks at five, and by seven, they were in a state of Bolivia. Together, the two were arrow dynamic, so off to Lost Wages they flew to tie the not.

Later the bride said, "Moe's art and the champagne caused me to let down my prohibitions" because no sooner had Ilse become an awfully wedded wife than Max contracted reptile dysfunction. Sadly, this led to the disillusion of the not, which was knot to be.

Eventually Ilse convinced herself that her relationship with Max, brief as it was, was a millstone. She vowed she would not bear falsies against another man, but the mesh is weak.

Once she regained cohesive speech, Ilse returned to the Autobahn Society, but the tacks of life seemed to exasperate her problems. "Perhaps it is my density," she mused. Though there were no longer any stigmata associated with divorce, she found it difficult to get off the dreadmill and the biddy pot. At first she suspected PBS, but this bout lasted longer than the customary week. "If only I had ESPN," she mused. At her lowest point, she considered rush-in roulette but got a taboo on her butt instead. A torn chili's tendon and a spinal-chord injury followed in quick secession. Eventually, she was diagnosed with bucolic plague, a rare form of the slime flu. Forced to take the anecdote, she checked herself into the Henry Ford Clinic, where people in her condition coagulate.

She was on tenderhooks for several weeks, but one of the duly constipated authorities gave her a Heimlich Remover, and that seemed to purge her system of everything but a migrating headache and the poultrygeist knocking around in her belfry.

Once free of the clinic, she ran off with a faith dealer on the sperm of the moment and threw off the yolk of her depression. "Yahweh!" she shouted waving the New Testicle. "I feel like Jesus climbing Calgary!" In one fatal swoop, Ilse had found the Holy Host and was forever waived.

II.

When Cucumber Vines Tangle with the Concubines

The first time I telephoned Sue, she, suspecting an interior motive, said, "I'm not interesting." But, of course, she was. And so was her mother, a person of gender, who told me once that New York needs a way to purge the effluent from their den of inequity. And when I asked Sue's father what he did for a living, he said he mounted bugs in the NYU etymology lab.

My German-American parents were similarly afflicted with what the Germans call *Zungensalat* or "tongue salad." Mother was forever yelling at me to shut the scream door, and Father worried I wasn't getting enough Arabic exercise. For the most part, our mixed greens left us congenially dysfunctional. But when the Katz family, our Jewish neighbors, overheard mother say, "It's time to Judenize the *Katze*," they accused us of being "rabbit racists." As Mother said, "With neighbors like these, who needs anemones?" Eventually, we were forced to leave the Lower East Side, naked as jaywalkers, and like Walt Whitman, take a fairy to Brooklyn.

It was here that I met Sue, my altar ego with the

photogenic memory, and began my schooling. I did my best to read between the academic tea leaves, but I was never the clown prince. Sue, who felt life has too much realism, loved my antics, but in a mostly Italian neighborhood, my family felt like social piranhas. Eventually the bias spread to my high school, where in the tenth grade, I was suspended when my teacher poised the following: "Who were our floundering fathers?" Well, that's what I thought she said, and that's why I answered, "Milton Pearl and Minnie Berle."

The teacher charged me with caricature assassination, and the principle agreed in principal, so I was sent to nomad's land. A few weeks later, the principle relaxed and said I might be readmitted after a conference with a parent or a cardigan. Sporting a new sweater, my father tried to explain how you can't get blood from a termite, which may or may not have helped my case.

After returning to school, I sang the "Bronze Lullaby" in chorus, toned my abominable muscles in PE, built a model of the Sixteenth Chapel for art, and wrote an essay on Tolstoyevsky's *War and Punishment* for English. I even convinced my journalism teacher that "grocery store" is redumnant. From a tough school off Flattush Avenue, I graduated *magnum cum laude*.

That summer, I proposed to Sue under the crapapple tree in her backyard. I also proposed that we splurge our savings until I could open a business. I knew it would be feast or salmon for a while especially since we had no savings to pool, but I didn't want her working as a cocktail mattress, which was her dream.

One day, a dyked-out clerk asked if I wanted paper or plastic, and I said, "I don't care—I'm bisacksual." Once and a while you get lucky in strife, and this was my turn: the store manager overheard what I'd said and offered me a job. He was planning to open a small restaurant in a corner of his grocery, "Custard's Last Stand," and he thought I'd be a good wit.

Given that the Ivory League wasn't calling, I accepted. When we opened, the menu featured everything from baked Nebraska to sweat and sour pork. On the breakfast menu, we offered tea and strumpets, and for the kids, we gave away pink insulation on a cardboard stick. A year later, thinking business was booming, I asked the boss to garnish my celery, but he fired me for my nerve. I don't want to cast any asparagus, but urbanite that he was, he didn't know Black and Gus from a Black Angus.

It was just as well, for I had ground my last beast and fried my last thighs. When I came home, Sue was curled up in the feeble position, saying she was closed for altercations until further notice. It seems the conundrums I'd been using had been recalled by the Sturgeon General. At any rate, we soon had to call a middle wife to cut the umbrella cord. Sue said she wanted a pre-natal agreement, but I said that train had sailed.

After the baby was born, Sue looked pale and emancipated. Based on antidotal information, we decided it was post-nasal depression. A Pabst beer confirmed our diagnosis, and two aspergillums in a glass of water helped her feel better.

Then like a massage from God, instead of the disillusion of our marriage I'd feared, the baby cured my channel vision, and I went fourth. I knew better than to put all my eggs in one basketball, so I took two jobs which required little speech: by day, I ran a valley-parking service; by night, I ran a mangled-care facility. Pretending to be moot was exhausting, but I eventually became a business typhoon.

Sue and I weren't ready for hostage care just yet. At last, in the proper frame of mind, we had learned how to hide our half-hazard errors.

The Gravity of Names: Names and Fate

"Your parents' love for each other is expressed in your life; their love for you is expressed in your name."—*The Wordspinner*

"The hand God deals you represents determinism. The way you play your cards represents free will."—*Norman Cousins*

The Romans used to say, "*Nomen ist omen*," or loosely translated, a name foretells the fate of that which bears it. Rolf Mengele, the "angel of death's son," once confessed, "I would have preferred a different father," or at least a different surname. Life cannot have been easy for the Austrian son of the man who conducted sadistic experiments at Auschwitz. One wonders why he didn't change his name. I know of one American who adopted his German wife's surname when they married. The young man was so ashamed of the 2003 invasion of Iraq that he moved to Europe and renounced all connections to his native heath.

Changing a name, it seems, is a form of burning bridges and lengthening the remaining roads. A German friend of ours divorced her husband when she discovered that he was having an affair. The betrayed mother of four took the bulk of his vast wealth and formally changed her name from "Frau Julia Bayer" to "Fräulein Julia Bay." She then purchased a ticket on a luxury liner and since then has rarely spent any time on land. Once in port, I asked her if she was so determined to erase all reminders of her husband why she had retained three letters of his name. She said she wanted people to know that, "*Er ist weg*," ("He is gone"). Of course, only those who knew her as a "Bayer" will ever understand the sleight of hand, but then revenge never made anyone rational.

Indeed, naming is often irrational as when the Poole family named their daughter "Sessie Ann," while behind her back, people called her "Sess Poole." Try that form of child abuse in Germany, and there's an excellent chance the name will be rejected by a council that oversees such matters. In the misguided name of freedom, however, Americans allow such parental malfeasance. I'm just guessing, but perhaps the Pooles were trying to revive the ancient custom of giving children apotropaic names, or unappealing labels to ward off evil. "Oedipus" is the classic example, for what God or mortal would be drawn to a child named "Big Foot"? As it turned out, many demons were drawn to the Sphinx slayer, including his mother who pierced the boy's feet and later married him.

I stumbled on the apotropaic class of names when our daughter's teacher invited me to tell her first graders the origins of their names. She sent a copy of the class roll home, and I went to work in my dictionaries. I had warned the teacher that some surnames, especially the Jewish ones, are unflattering, so I told her I would only deal with given names that disguised "a little fairy princess" or "a blessed gift of God." My carefully laid plans, however, went awry when I came to "Cameron Kennedy" whose full Scotch-Irish name (he has no middle name) means "crooked-nosed boy with an ugly head." I could just imagine thirty six-year-olds laughing as poor Cameron sobbed at his desk. So when the time came for me to reveal the embarrassing name, which I'd saved for last, I apologized and said I'd been unable to find anything.

"Booooo," the class intoned until I said I *had found* their teacher's name.

"What is it?" they demanded rising to their feet.

"Rebecca, your teacher, was originally a woman who cleaned the cow stalls." At six, anything remotely resembling a fart joke brings the house down, so I ended on that classy note.

Life would be much easier for name researchers if everyone had a name like Mozart's. Apparently Leopold and Anna Maria were determined to raise a God-loving human because their son's birth register reads, "Joannes Chrysostomus Wolfgangus Theophilus Gottlieb Mozart." No, I did not omit "Amadeus"; that was adopted later. The name he was christened with means, "John the Golden Wolfgang, God-loving, God-loving Mozart." Apparently, part of the boy's adolescent rebellion included altering his name to "Wolfgang Amadeo," which morphed into "Amade," which morphed into "Amadeus," but regardless of the spelling, "Amadeus," "Theophilus," and "Gottlieb" all mean, "God-loving." In other words, whether the deity reads Latin, Greek, or German, He will know that Mozart is His golden-haired boy.

The question though is did the name shape the composer? Or, is his music heavenly because his name reiterates his allegiance to God? Of course not, but one is given pause when studying the wonderful list of names that John Train collected for his 1977 book, *Remarkable Names of Real People*. Among Train's discoveries are Cardinal Sin, the Archbishop of Manila, and A. Moron, the Commissioner of Education in the Virgin Islands. I imagine these two men striving all their lives to prove their names wrong. Apparently, as their titles indicate, both succeeded. Then there's Linda Whynot, a prostitute; a Mr. Vice, who was arrested 890 times; and a Dr. Ufelter, a gynecologist. Though I'm a firm believer in human free will, I can imagine young Dr. Ufelter toying with various specialties before the gravity of his name pulled him into the orbit of his eventual specialty. For every patient who thinks Dr. Ufelter is making light of a serious subject, there's probably another who thinks he's just in lockstep with his God-chosen destiny.

John Hobbes thought that people often make a neat pile of their mistakes and then create a scapegoat called fate. A case in point is Philander Rodman. Philander Sr. abandoned Philander Jr., who abandoned Dennis, the basketball star, who married himself because no one loved him more. As I write, Junior has twenty-seven children by four wives and untold girlfriends. Though Philander Jr. has tried, one shouldn't blame a name (regardless of its suggestiveness) for a lifetime of infidelity.

Brand and business names, however, are a different story. In the forty years that I have lived in the South Carolina upstate, I have seen the following businesses rise and fall: The Greasy Spoon in Anderson, complete with a sign showing grease dripping from a spoon; Chili Bordello, a Mexican restaurant not far from Greenville's Bob Jones University; Montezuma's Revenge, a Mexican restaurant in Seneca; and Smaragda's Table in Clemson. The later was a short-lived Greek restaurant that was really quite good, but few who read the sign by the highway knew what it was. I confided my fears in Smaragda and her husband one night, and they just laughed. Nevertheless, I'm convinced that the owners of these four restaurants either wanted their ventures to fail or they did not understand that irony and mystery are inappropriate when foreign food is involved.

I am also convinced that names like The Boom-Boom Room, a Simpsonville bar where a man was shot recently, have a gravitational field of their own. I realized this thirty years ago when I read of a boy who jumped 150 feet to his death into Lake Jocassee about twenty miles north of here. The road leading to the site of the boy's last decision is still called Jumping Off Rock Road. In my estimation, it's criminal.

Fanny Assingham's Offspring: Misnomers and Ill-Gotten Names

"Many ... have names that sound like pharmaceuticals. Take my family, for example: my name is Advil. This is my wife Cloret. Here's is my son Tylenol. Hold it down, Tylenol; you're giving me a headache." —*Darrell Savad*

"A good name is better than a precious ointment." —*Ecclesiastes*

Don't get the wrong idea, but I seem to be drawn to men with unisex names. One of these named Claire went for an MRI recently to see about some abdominal-area pain. A few days later, the doctor who'd read the scans called and said, "I'm sorry, Ma'am, but we have not been able to locate your uterus."

"Perhaps," said the patient, "my lawyer can explain that *Mr.* Claire Casson doesn't have one."

Then there's Col. Beverly Sterrit. Though he had the good sense to take "Ben" as a nickname, the army took slight notice of it. After his release from a Japanese POW camp in 1945, the army reassigned him to Ft. Benning. He reported to his new quarters and discovered to his delight that they were in the WAC billets. The female NCO in charge directed him to the bachelor officer's quarters, but Beverly pulled rank on the sergeant and stayed until the MPs escorted him away.

Evelyn Waugh (whose first wife was also an Evelyn), Erich Maria von Weber (it's a Catholic tradition to honor the Virgin), Florenz Ziegfield (who was married to Billie Burke), Tracy Morgan, Morgan Freeman, and scores of others like epicene "Pat" on *Saturday Night Live* struggled through life with an androgynous name. A study done in 2008 concluded that American boys with names like Alexis, Osama, and Emigdio (unisex, threatening, and foreign respectively) are more likely to end up in jail. But there are worse fates than prison. One fellow christened "Donald Duck" by his clueless parents committed suicide after moving to civilization only to discover that he bore the same name as a popular cartoon character with an odd voice and no pants.

In H.G. Wells' novel *Kipps* (1905), a male character is convinced that nine of ten girls named "Euphemia" will come to no good. Apparently, he assumed that the added pressure of carrying a saint's name through life is more than the "weaker vessels" can bear. That's pure speculation, of course, but when Houston Natural Gas and InterNorth merged in 1985, someone should have been shot. Lippincott & Margulies, a respected New York brand-producer, was hired to cobble "Enteron" out of "InterNorth" and "Houston," but apparently no one opened a dictionary. L & M's house of cards went up in smoke when someone smelled something and lit a match, for "enteron" refers to that other natural-gas supplier known as the gastrointestinal tract. L & M's second choice was "Enron," and my guess is that you know the rest of the story. A bad name, it seems, often subverts the entire enterprise especially when crooks are running the show.

A few miles from where I write, Bad Creek flows into a reservoir that Duke Power uses to generate electricity for the grid. Despite the "poverty of [American] nomenclature," as Thoreau charged, Bad Creek is fed by Wuss Creek, and Wuss Creek is fed by Wusser Creek. The farther into the mountain laurel the pioneers pushed, the worse they found the vegetation, the slope, the soil, or all three, thus the uphill progression of names. But these three are distinctive and colorful, and I would not change them. However, I would think twice before moving to Fucking, Austria or even Intercourse, PA.

Many change their name when they think they have out grown them. About 1525, Philippus Aureolus Theophrastus Bombastus von Hohenheim (literally "horse-loving golden boy, divine speaker with a bombastic tendency from a home on high") changed his name to "Paracelsus." Why the change? His over-stuffed name holds a clue: after his discoveries of zinc and laudanum's therapeutic values, Philippus thought that he was "beyond Celsus," the Roman encyclopedist, and he wished to let the rest of the world know what he thought of himself.

More often, people just get tired of their ancestors' little joke (advertent or inadvertent) and pay the court fee to make a change. When George Nutt earned a degree in psychiatry, he changed his surname to McNulty, retaining only three letters of his birthright. In hindsight, I'd say he made a smart choice.

Often the change is political as when Malcolm Little realized that his surname commemorated people who once held his American ancestors in bondage. As soon as he was able, he changed his name to "Malcolm X" to acknowledge his unknown African ancestors.

While politics are ephemeral, the actions taken in its name are harder to erase. For three decades, Iraqi parents named their sons "Saddam Hussein" to receive the equivalent of $200 for the homage they'd paid to their wealthy, arrogant leader. But less than a year after the dictator was overthrown, there were over three hundred people waiting to have "Saddam Hussein" changed to anything but the name they bore.

Finally there's the forced change. When James L.

Stewart began making films, he realized there was already a "James Stewart" on the Hollywood payroll, so the studio made him change his name, and James L. Stewart became "Stewart Granger." To friends, he remained "Jimmy," however, which only increased the confusion.

Many have names, however, that they should have changed but did not. There are hundreds of names like "Shitz," "Fuckart," "Titley," and "Shoebottom" in American telephone directories. Family pride and sheer stubbornness surely must figure into the decisions to retain eyebrow-lifting names. When people like Jane (not her real name) Dover discovered she was pregnant, what possessed her to name her daughter "Aileen Dover" to commemorate the conception? What were the parents of Viola Unstrung, Fair Hooker, and Butch Faggot thinking when they tied a dead albatross around the necks of their children? The Germans avoid such embarrassments with a name registry that reviews new names. But like any board with authority, power went to their head, and instead of just quashing names like "Ima Hogg," they refused to let German parents choose non-Germanic names like Sasha without a lengthy court battle. Since reforms in 2006, matters have moderated, but one still looks in vain for German children named "Yuri" or "Yoko."

Americans are far too defensive of their freedom to name, so I will not suggest any guidelines for choosing or creating good personal names beyond, "Avoid naming your children after tyrants, demons, and gods." Business names are a different kettle of squirrel. One email I received in 2011 showed photographs of Stoner Drug, S&M Tree Service, Prom Discount Liquors, and PMS Firearms. From the looks of the establishments, business did not appear to be good. From someone who never took a course in economics, here are six business-wise suggestions.

- The Gingko Tree Service throws too narrow a net.
- American Enterprise, Inc. throws too vague and broad a net.
- The Girdle Garage is insensitive to its customers.
- OK Service is insensitive to itself.
- Fuchs Lubricants is in denial thinking no one will be offended.
- The Pizza Privy forgets that imagination is one key to appetite.

Finally there are the true misnomers. Despite their time-honored names, peanuts are legumes, fireflies are beetles, horned toads are lizards, and Douglass firs are pines. Often, however, the truth of the matter is more obscure: who would suspect that the Pennsylvania Dutch are really German, that Rocky Mountain oysters are calf testicles, and Old Ironsides has flanks of oak, twenty-one inches thick?

I've read that there's an East Asian ESL text titled *Correctly English in 100 Days*. Clearly a hundred days is not enough to master our complex mistress. As for me, keep the bad judgments and inaccuracies coming; their faults help me love her all the more.

A Fig Leaf for Dr. Bowdler: Obscenity

"If God heard every shepherd's curse, all our sheep would be dead."
—*Russian proverb*

"Do we really want a language in which we 'gosh darn the torpedoes'?" —*Anonymous*

To answer the inquisitor above: "Hell no," and here's why.

On Dec. 7, 1941 as church bells summoned the faithful to churches across Honolulu, the Japanese began their attack on US ships anchored in the harbor. From the loudspeakers on the *USS Oklahoma* came the following, "Man your battle stations, goddamn it! This is no shit!" Instantly, the sailors who heard this command understood it was not a drill. The percussive shock issued from the bridge, however, was no match for the enemy torpedoes exploding below the water line, and the great battleship was soon sunk. Had the captain's expletives come a few minutes earlier, there's a fair chance the ship would have survived.

Yet just five years earlier, David O. Selznick had paid a $5000 fine for using "damn" in *Gone with the Wind*. Never mind that the word had appeared in the novel, and thousands of Americans had read it before watching the movie.

One might conclude from the two examples above that profanity has a place in a theater of war but not a theater on Main Street. If that is your take, you'd be mistaken. Victorian censors who sliced and diced *The Red Badge of Courage* insisted that a mortally wounded soldier should say, "By Jiminy, I've been shot." It's safe to say Crane's tone-deaf editors had never heard a dying human's scream.

Granted there are exceptions. For the last twenty years, my wife and I have employed a Mennonite man to inspect our furnace before we turn on the gas in the fall. After his work under the house had been completed on a recent visit, Hans told me about some eye surgery he'd had. Nearing the end of the procedure, my devout friend realized to his horror that the anesthetic was wearing off. Pressing a fist to his eye, he said, "I wanted to tell the surgeon to go to 'H,' but he was sewing my eye shut at the time." He allowed his voice to rise a few decibels telling me the story, but he never told the surgeon, "I feel your needle piercing my eyeball," nor did he puzzle him with "Go to hell." He just bit his tongue. Of course, many if not most of us would have been pleading for morphine and spewing un-dingbatted maledicta. Perhaps most remarkable is the euphemism "H" for *hell* that even the soul-cautious Puritans would have smirked at.

A brief historical overview might be helpful to show how in the name of free speech most Western vocabularies have become more tolerant of the profane as the East rushes futilely to plug the locks at Suez. When the Normans defeated the Anglo-Saxons in 1066, the four-letter words most speakers of English still think of as off limits in polite society became taboo. "Shit" turned to "excrement" virtually overnight in evolutionary linguistic terms. In 1350, a conviction for blasphemy resulted in the loss of one lip; the second conviction took the other lip, and a third took the tongue. Nearly four hundred years later, the strongest oath uttered in the King James Bible was, "The devil take you." Little had changed by the mid-seventeenth century when a child caught swearing at his parents risked being executed. In the late nineteenth century, literature explaining the rhythm method was equivalent to pornography in the eyes of the law. But when Joyce's *Ulysses* was exonerated in 1933, Judge Woolsey concluded that the novel was an "emetic," not an "aphrodisiac." Today, the phrase "not bloody likely," which caused an uproar when *Pygmalion* debuted in 1912, barely lifts an eyebrow. And "pissed," considered vulgar as late as 1980, was unapologetically used in a *Newsweek* headline in 2011.

Indeed, "pissed" in the sense of "incensed" has enjoyed a renaissance in recent years though John Wycliffe and the King James translators thought the punchier "piss" polite enough to include in 2 Kings 18:27. After the KJV, however, "urine," "waste," and "water" prevailed in translations the way "dung," "filth," and "excrement" took the high ground from Wycliffe's "turds" in 1384. The rise and fall of words like "bloody" can give readers who dip into the past vertigo. Try to explain this: "fuck" was excluded from the first edition of the *Oxford English Dictionary*, but "windfucker," a bird capable of hovering, was not.

An interesting sub-category of obscenity includes words that appear obscene but are not and never have been. Take the following sentence, "When Delores issued a papal bull, Dick dropped his joystick, left their bungalow, and drove off in his wife's Volvo to buy some shiitakes and kumquats." Who, I ask, would deny poor Emily Dickinson a good frigate?

A sub-sub category consists of words that few suspect have an off-color element in their lineage. Who eats a buttered slice of pumpernickel anymore thinking, "This hard, dark German delicacy is going to make me pass wind like the devil?" but "fart like the devil" is what the word means at its roots. Who uses a pencil and is reminded of a penis, attends a seminar and connects it to semen, gives testimony while holding one's testicles, or sings of partridges in pear trees thinking of farting birds? Okay, I do, but it keeps me off the streets.

Finally, there's the euphemistic category. Tired and cold, our Mennonite furnace man quoted above might bring himself to say, "Geez Louise, what the Sam Hill happened to that cotton pickin' sombitch?" What he means is, "Jesus Christ, where the hell is my damn screwdriver?" If he's talking to himself, how can I object, but if he's trying to communicate to a co-worker, my guess is that he's failed.

✻

My defense of obscenity has a sound psychological pedigree. In 1781, Denis Diderot cured his wife's "vapors" by reading pornography to her. Taking note of that a century later, Freud argued that civilization began when the first human uttered a brickbat instead of hurling one, or said "Fuck you" instead of penetrating his foe's anus. But when Earl Long swore freely on Louisiana public television in 1959, his wife had him committed to the state asylum for the insane. Earl, however, continued to swear and had the asylum's superintendent fired, for Earl was still governor. About 1960, the linguist Allen Walker Read opined that the use of "defecate" instead of "shit" by anyone over twenty in the company of his or her friends is "indicative of grave mental health." Indeed, there's therapeutic value in judiciously releasing the ooze of the lizard brain where obscenity resides. Indeed, stuttering may be overcome by cursing, and suffering is eased.

Aesop's ancient warning about crying wolf, however, still holds, for it has been shown that women who suddenly start cursing in childbirth suffer less pain than men in surgery. Overuse often nullifies the anesthetic effect, which is what happened when the *New Yorker* in 2011 gratuitously referred to an intimidating chronometer as "a don't-fuck-with-me" watch.

Giving with One Hand, Taking with the Other: Paradox

"God made everything out of the void, but the void shines through." —*Paul Valery*

"Anyone who isn't confused doesn't really understand the situation." —*Edward R. Murrow*

Miksa, an only child whose name means "the one between," was raised by parents who forbade sweets and rewarded him with Eskimo Pies. In the winter, he ate blubber by the light of a beeswax candle; in the summer, he ate honey by the light of a whale-oil lantern.

His father, Pukiq, the tribe's over-achieving undertaker, brought a refrigerator home one day explaining that it would keep the milk from freezing. Further south, he said, the haunted boxes were used to keep the milk from becoming cheese. "The machine's like your breath—it thaws your frozen fingers even as it cools your soup."

When Miksa's parents went seal hunting, the lad stayed with one of his grandmothers. One told him, "What will be will be." The other said, "Life is what you make of it." Miksa often returned home with a headache, which his father said was a form of freezer burn. "Same difference," he said.

When Miksa turned sixteen, Pukiq cornered him in the igloo and said, "You're free to do as you must, son. It's time for you to get untracked." So they went outside where the father showed him how to build a toasty shelter from packed snow. "Now for the hundredth time, I'm not going to repeat myself, so pay attention. You may think we are riding the bipolar express around here, but sometimes you have to plan to be spontaneous. You know, think outside the box while coloring within the lines. Take this dome," he said, "the more snow I pile on it, the stronger it becomes. Snow is like salt—it can kill or preserve. I trust you know that the icebergs in Norton Bay are fresh, but the water they're floating in can kill you. You must learn the difference. Life's a puzzle, Miksa—when one of the dogs dies in the traces, it falls down; when a seal dies, it 'falls' up. Animals know how to live and die instinctively. If humans don't want to learn, nothing can stop them."

Miksa, therefore, made up his mind to discover why things not worth mentioning were discussed at considerable length. After flying from Koyuk to Fairbanks, he thumbed a ride to Seattle with a compassionate conservative named Dark Starr who told his passenger, "The more the merrier, but three's a crowd." Starr was on his way south because he was "head over heels in love" with a girl from Portland. "When I came to Dead Horse to make my fortune in the oil fields," said Starr with a smile, "I figured 'out of sight out of mind,' but 'absence made my heart grow fonder.'"

A few hours down the Alcan Highway, a Mountie pulled alongside Starr and motioned him to the side of the road. "Young man," he said, "I clocked you doing close to a hundred on that last hill."

"I could care less," said Starr, "but tell me, how can I break the law of Canada while obeying the laws of physics?"

"Son, you have a right to do anything on this road that I cannot see," said the officer with a black belt in yoga as he wrote the ticket.

After Starr calmed down, Miksa asked his Republican friend why he'd left home in the first place. "My parents!" said Starr. "Like the Marines, they were never at peace unless they were fighting. One Saturday night, Dad came home drunk and battered my Mom. They x-rayed her head

163

and found nothing, but she was never the same. Although she'd been drinking with her slam-dancing boyfriend, the judge gave Dad twenty years. When he was paroled two years later, all he ever said was, 'Why did your mother leave me to raise you?' The dissonance was deafening, so I split. The last thing Dad told me was, 'The furthest way out is the nearest way home.' I'm still trying to wrap my head around that one." But Miksa understood.

At daybreak, Starr dropped his passenger at a Seattle hotel and headed south. As the car drove off, the Inuit lad noticed Starr's bumper sticker for the first time, "Honk if you love peace and quiet." The sign on the hotel's revolving door also boded well, "Members and Non-members Only." A poster in the lobby touted an upcoming concert—Percy Sledge and the Love Tractor.

After checking in, Miksa walked up the down escalator to his room. He slept for a few hours and headed for the dining room, where the cook's specialty was "chicken soup for the vegetarian soul." Miksa sensed a kindred spirit. His name was Kaya, and he hailed from Barrow. As Miksa ate, he asked this fellow emigrant about job opportunities. "You appear to know nothing," said the cook, "and could care less. I'd say China Mart is your best bet."

"Well, here goes nothing," said Miksa pushing himself back from the table.

The first sign he saw in the cavernous store said, "Buy one at twice the price, and get the second free." Miksa immediately felt at home and was hired to sell appliances because he understood the psychic sumo of refrigerators. Minutes later, the new sales associate confided to a customer that a China Mart vacuum cleaner would "cut his work in half."

"Good," said the customer, "I'll take two."

The store manager, who'd overheard this transaction, thought, "At last, a hire who can lead by walking behind. Management material!" But a week later, our hero was fired in Beijing's effort to spare no expense in cutting costs. Before he left, he was instructed to train his replacement.

Though Miksa understood that we're all in this together by ourselves, he eventually returned to Koyuk, where he'd learned to smell the roses while staying off the grass. Pukiq greeted him saying, "Son, you are the exception that proves the rule. Welcome home!"

Expecting a surprise, our poor prodigal realized there was none, which didn't surprise him.

Driving Forward While Looking Back: The Past

"Henry Ford thought history was bunk but built a ninety-acre museum to house it."—*The Wordspinner*

"I increasingly find that the past is where I most want to be." — *Roger Rosenblatt*

On the banks of the Little River, stand the rusting and rotting remains of Newry, South Carolina, population 172. This former mill town, *circa*. 1894, is what I imagine Clemson would look like if the university folded. Less than ten miles from here, Newry is well off the beaten two-lane; indeed, many around here tell me they've never heard of it. After reading about it in the early 1970s, I took the family on a Sunday drive to see the town that time has disowned sitting in the sepia shadow of a hundred-foot-tall earthen dam. I don't think we've been back since.

Driving along at walking speed, I was telling our two children about the company towns that often sprang up along rivers following the Civil War, and how mill owners often extorted the labor of twelve-year-old children from their employees. No work, no house, no groceries was the implied motto. I said the opposition to learning in these towns was only matched by slave owners a few generations earlier who forbade the "edge tools" known as reading and writing. Uppity slaves were occasionally punished with another "edge tool," used to sever hand or head.

As I turned a corner near the shuttered mill, I slowed to a stop before a half dozen adolescents who were loitering in the middle of the road. One young woman with smoke wafting from her nostrils sauntered over to my side of the car, so I rolled the window down to see what she wanted. "Whadda *you* lookin' at?" she inquired. Her tone and a long drag on her cigarette indicated more of what she meant than her words, so without replying, I eased around the teens, locked the doors, and headed home. For this young woman, as William Faulkner said, "the past is not dead; it's not even past."

Guardians of a heritage frequently assume a self-justifying posture. I recall a former student growing increasingly defensive as he explained how he and his cohorts in butternut gray starved themselves to look "more realistic" as they "refought" Civil War battles on the weekends. Today, the mill at Newry has not finished any cotton in thirty years, and the future for those who are staying must seem grim. The darker that light grows, the better the past seems. But how good could it have been if children were tending the looms, blacks were considered subhuman, homosexuals were felons, women could not draw their own pay checks, life expectancy was about fifty, and no one had air conditioning?

As a species, we are divided when it comes to our past. Roman Catholic priests often say, "He who looks back is not worthy of God's Kingdom." Napoleon thought history was "just a set of lies society had agreed on." James Joyce thought it was the "nightmare" he was struggling to awake from. And the forward-thinking architect Frank Lloyd Wright reportedly had his car's rear window covered and mirrors removed because he wasn't interested in where he'd been.

Across the aisle sit those like Marcel Proust who thought the past was "paradise." Samuel Coleridge was somewhat less generous imagining it as "a lantern on the stern." In the last century, Norman Cousins came to regard antiquity as a "vast early warning system." Various writers have thought we should pay more attention to Cousin's radar because one day we'll all be spending a lot of time there. Those ignorant of history often praise it, reasoning that it had to be better because nothing could be worse than the present and what we can forecast of the future.

Returning to Faulkner's notion of a past that never passes, I remember a retired colleague who volunteered to tutor an Afghan student preparing for her master's orals in English. We all knew she had risked her life to get here and that her family had been targeted by the Taliban, but we also knew there were yawning holes in her knowledge of British and American literature. Preparing to discuss *Moll Flanders*, my colleague said, "Now this novel may give you trouble because it's set in the eighteenth century." Said the student, "You forget, professor, that I come from the eighteenth century." She probably meant the thirteenth, but what's five hundred years?

Quaint as it might be for a country to exist in any century but the current one, it was simply unacceptable to the Taliban that this woman wanted to escape her "heritage." It's unthinkable to many Muslim fundamentalists that she might drag her country to the present, but it's also inhuman that she might have acid splashed on her face for receiving an education.

Given that my German wife marched in the 1000th anniversary of her home town in 1952, she was amused when Clemson University made such a bother over its centennial in 1993. The oldest section of Helmstedt, her home town, has a number of *Fachwerk* homes with points of pride engraved in the lintels. One reads, "Giordano Bruno lived here 1507-09." A few doors further, another reads, "Poet Hoffman von Fallersleben, who wrote the words to the German national anthem, lived here 1581-83." Next door, another reads, "Anno Domini 1567, nothing much happened here." Below that is a carving of a cap-n-bell, the symbol of Till Eulenspiegel, the legendary German prankster/humorist. This home owner with a sense of humor, of course, is referring to the sheer tedium of most human lives. Just think what boast you might carve over your own door that would still draw visitors in five hundred years.

Tedious as it might have been, it's fair to assume that most of our ancestors were doing the best they could under often trying circumstances. We also need to remember that history is always an over-simplification. Take Gen. Sherman's five-week march to the sea in 1864: we have at least fifty extant journals that record every day of the march. And that's one campaign in a single war. Recently, the Library of Congress announced that it had become the archive for Twitter, a collection which grows by a factor of fifty million every day.

Given numbers like these, it is understandable that every culture uses the wind to sort the grain from the chaff. A Nepalese fifth grader told me in 2011 that she can see Mt. Everest from her home. To make conversation, I asked her if she knew who first climbed that mountain.

"Tenzing Norgay!" she announced proudly. "I've seen his statue in Darjeeling."

"Have you ever heard of Sir Edmund Hillary?" I wondered.

"No, sir," she said as innocently as any westerner who's never heard of Tenzing Norgay, Hillary's Sherpa guide and porter.

With all the wisdom mascara provides, Tammy Faye Bakker thought neither individual nor nation could advance "looking in the rearview mirror." On the contrary, I frequently check my car's mirrors to see if anything is uncomfortably close especially on two-lane, mountain highways. If there is, I blink my turn signal at the crest of the next hill to let the speedier traveler know it's safe to pass. This is not to say I live in the past: like Mordecai Kaplan, I give it a vote, not a veto, for when we bronze yesterday, no one including the dog can swallow it.

From Fluffy Feathers to Plucked Fowl: Pornography

"Skip the woo,
cut to screw,
nothing's true." —*The Wordspinner*

"Pornography is in the groin of the beholder." —Anonymous

A friend who collects old postcards showed me one printed about 1900 that had him puzzled. Over the caption, "An Owl Can String Me," is a black-and-white photograph of a woman with pinned-up hair seated on a slat-back chair. She's fully dressed but has crossed her legs revealing a shapely ankle in black stockings. Indeed, the only skin she reveals are her forearms, hands, and a coy face. "Suitors," however, should not despair, for one of her high-topped shoes is untied, and she is casually pointing to the loose lace. So, is this an innocent picture, or is she saying in the heavily coded language of Victoria's day, "Honey, it's wine o'clock"?

Given the date, I'd argue it's a "French postcard" even though the text is English. As I interpret both kit and boodle here, the woman is saying, "The lonely nocturnal hunter is invited to lace me up or lace me down and then have his way with me." The card is, in other words, the first of E. L. James's fifty shades of gray and, thus, may be worth a fortune.

In 2013, it's trite to say that values regarding pornography have changed over the last century; indeed, without these changes, the following events would have been unthinkable. In the spring of 1999, a female student had herself whipped by classmates in "Pornography: The Writing of Prostitutes," an English course taught at Connecticut's Wesleyan University. This behavior was in partial fulfillment of the requirement to "make your own pornography without constraint." When the inevitable complaints landed on the president's desk, the school issued the following statement: "…The student was dressed in slacks but no blouse. At her invitation, some of her classmates did—hesitantly, feebly, and to the general amusement of everyone—gently whip her. No members of the class were at risk. Nothing more serious than ideas were at stake."

Now, I've never taught a class in pornography, but it does surprise me that the school took no issue with the student stripping down to her slacks and a leather harness that left her "mostly topless," as one journalist put it, in a co-ed class. Call me prudish, but such tolerance is unbefitting a respectable university. I may be alone, but I still believe *some* control of Eros is a duty of the state as well as the individual.

We can argue until the cows come to roost over the correspondence of sail and ballast, but I'm not an absolutist when it comes to freeing anything from tongues to zippers. Though consenting adults in private may "Sodom like there is no Gomorrah," in pornography some action is best left off-stage or at least with the lights turned down. As a poet, "indirection" is a word I live by.

"To be poor and physically unappetizing," Kenneth Tynan argued, "is to be sexually condemned to solitary confinement, from which pornography offers the illusion of release." Though Thomas Jefferson neglected to mention this, it is self-evident that everyone, rich or poor, appetizing or not, is entitled to some sexual satisfaction in their lives. However, this does not grant anyone the right to violence especially if that victim is a child. The majority of

Americans, myself included, applauded the US Supreme Court's decision in 1982 to make child pornography an exception to the First Amendment.

In an essay by Margaret Atwood, written after researching her novel *Bodily Harm*, she tells of men being sodomized with broomsticks and women having their nipples cut off in the name of free speech. As I said, what consenting adults do is none of the state's business, but these acts described by Atwood were neither consensual nor private because they were filmed and sold. If my opposition to such crimes marks me as square-toed, so be it. Unlike the Victorian woman described above, my laces are tied but loose.

William Blake thought "the road to excess leads to the palace of wisdom," but I find that gilding the lily, perfuming the violet, and purpling the prose are not merely unwise, but repellant. I'm shocked that abused women in this country wait until the 35th time on average before they call the police. And I am disappointed that while 66% of Americans think pornography is immoral, only 28% think the death penalty is. I call these two samples "statistical porn."

In recent years, some curious blooms have sprung up beside "the road to excess." These include gastroporn (eating sixty-nine hot dogs in ten minutes), porn for plants (videos of bees storming flowers), botanical porn (close-ups of agave plants), porn for women (pictures of men vacuuming), and eco-porn (nature filtered and colorized), but they all pale in comparison to "gorno," or war pornography. I recognize it when I don't get an erection.

The war porn I am referring to is not the prurient material the OSS considered dropping on the Eagle's Nest hoping Adolf Hitler, a borderline psychotic, would be pushed over the edge. Nor is it the lewd films the Israelis managed to broadcast over Palestinian television stations in 2002. I'm referring to the "home movies" from Iraq and Afghanistan which slithered onto the Internet beginning about 2003. One site posted pictures of severed and maimed limbs under the caption: "Guess which part this is?" Given this sadistic climate, the pictures of Americans humiliating Iraqi prisoners at Abu Ghraib should surprise no one.

We appear to be on a slippery slope whose middle ground we slid past several decades ago. In 1900, pictures of fully dressed women with flirty smiles were sold from beneath the counter. Today, "snuff films" thrust and counter-thrust against computer filters with unrelenting frequency. Sure, government censors worry me, but I worry more about people like Ted Bundy watching violent porn, and then acting on their fantasies. Bundy, you may remember, is the serial killer who said, "I've met a lot of men who were motivated to commit violence just like me. And without exception, without question, every one of them was deeply involved with pornography."

As a liberal minister used to say, "Sin with courage but restraint."

Timing the Rain Dance: Prayer

"Some Baptists have reasoned
that Jehovah does not
answer the prayer of a Jew.
Of course He did.
He said, 'No,'
but many did not hear." —*The Wordspinner*

"If you know you're praying, you're not praying right.
Black out the windows to see the light." —*The Wordspinner*

Though we worshipped the same god, I grew up in a family divided by prayer. My mother's Protestant parents in South Georgia prayed over most meals and taught their grandchildren to clasp their hands so that the right thumb crossed over its sinister companion. Furthermore, our grandmother instructed the girls to cross their legs when petitioning the deity. They weren't told why, but we figured it out in adolescence.

My father's father in Western Illinois was nominally a Presbyterian, yet he forced his wife to leave the Catholic Church before they wed. No one is sure, but Grandfather was apparently embarrassed by the Vatican's excommunication of his fiancée's church, which was in all the papers. At any rate, they eloped and were married in the parlor of a justice of the peace. However, in their fifty years together, they never attended a Protestant church that anyone can recall. After Grandfather died, my grandmother went right back to the church she'd been raised in. It was as a rejuvenated Catholic that she would turn a statue of St. Jude to the wall until her keys were located, but when meal time rolled around, she'd say, "For Christ's sake, let's eat!" To her credit, she didn't consider prayer a contraceptive; it was a millstone, she said, about the neck of pride.

My wife's Lutheran family dutifully paid their annual "church tax," but like my paternal grandparents, they rarely attended services. This is not to say that my mother-in-law lacked respect for God, but she wore her gratitude lightly and rarely invoked His name. She did not need to speak of angels and such because they were etched in her selfless behavior. However, among other things, she taught her children the following bedtime prayer: *"Lieber Gott, mach' mich fromm,/ daß ich in dem Himmel komm."* ("Dear God, make me pious, so I'll go to heaven.") As I read and translate these verses, the clause "if I die in my sleep" is understood.

Coincidentally, my mother taught her children a similar prayer, "Now I lay me down to sleep, I pray the Lord my soul to keep. If I should die before I wake, I pray the Lord my soul to take." Why parents think they should send their children to bed with a morbid reminder passes all understanding, but the intentions, I think, are pure. Indeed, we might all profit from more time on our knees.

Nevertheless, when I heard a cousin pray, "Now I lay me down to bed,/ dear God, bless my sleepy head," I knew I'd been robbed. Inspired by Roy Rogers, one of my boyhood idols, I changed my bedtime ritual to, "Until Roy, Daddy, and I meet again, may the good Lord take a likin' to me." Thinking about that lonely appeal now, it seems like a lot to ask, but someone was evidently pleased with me because I was sent to a cold war, not two hot ones like my father fought in.

My mother also taught her children gratitude in the form of this mealtime blessing, "God is great; God is good. Thank you, God, for this food. Amen." When our children were born, my wife and I decided we didn't want them raised in a denomination *we* had chosen, but we *did* want them to appreciate the humbling power of transcendental law. So we adopted a Native American blessing, "Great Spirit, grant that I may not criticize my neighbor until I have walked a mile in his moccasins." As best I can determine, that prayer has been answered more often than not.

One of my sisters, who eventually became a Methodist minister, admits now to practicing competitive prayer. When spending the night with her friends or cousins, Karen usually managed to stay on her knees longer than anyone else when the word came to, "Say your prayers." One of my cousins now says that she sensed Karen was destined for the seminary as evidenced by her callused knees. When our Mother died in 2008, the family drove to the Washington National Cathedral after the services at Arlington. It so happened that a canvas maze, modeled on the one in Chartres Cathedral, was on loan at the time, and visitors were welcome to walk it. Of course, Karen spent more time in mazeful meandering than anyone else.

Living just thirty miles from the brass knuckles on the fist of the Bible, a.k.a. Bob Jones University, I am often reminded of prayer by church signs in the front yard. One sign years ago informed me that "Moderation is a sin," but more recently I was reminded, "Delay is not denial." As a recent drought worsened, however, the sign changed to read, "Pray for the harvest, but keep hoeing the weeds."

The self-emancipated slave, Frederick Douglass came to understand the virtue of diligent hoeing on his own. He also said that he prayed for twenty years to be freed from his hoe and chains. When he finally realized that the deity has a universe to manage, he said after forging his emancipation papers, "I prayed with my legs." With hands and feet now free, he helped to raise an army that broke the chains of thousands.

Shortly after the Civil War ended, Francis Galton, the British statistician, began hearing stories of parrots trained to pray, "God save the queen." He did the math and determined that despite millions praying for Victoria, she and her predecessors did not live any longer than the woman or man in the street. Along these lines, a theology professor said that if God answered every shepherd's curse, the sheep would soon be dead. On the other hand, the professor said, if God answered every prayer for a sick loved-one, Earth would soon resemble an algae-clotted pond.

⁂

For years, I thought of prayer as a single-pointed ladder leaning precariously against the wall of heaven—a ladder left in the orchard long after all the fruit had been picked. I was of the same mind as those who placed their faith in airbags and multivitamins. However, I gradually came to understand prayer's potential as auto-psychotherapy—a dialogue between my better and lesser natures. It often begins, "Great Spirit, help me to be the person my wife and others need me to be." This places me among the 20% of American agnostics who pray daily.

For all my belief, however, nothing shook my faith more than the report that my wife required a mastectomy. Ever since the surgery, we have made the long drive south for her check-ups, and for twenty-seven years now, she has been cancer-free. My supporting role in the Emory-clinic ritual consists of waiting with several turbaned women and their husbands in the lobby. Here we sit thumbing the well-worn magazines, drinking tea from cardboard cups, and fingering our silent rosaries in petitionary prayer. When I see Ingrid's smile as she returns to the lobby through the "breast-imaging" door, I know our "lease" has been renewed. A prayer of thanks is the least I can offer. Indeed, "thank you" becomes our shared mantra as we rediscover our way home.

The Canonical Martini: Quality

"The barn owl hoots as she hunts the field
so that tomorrow it will also yield." —*The Wordspinner*

"Some say the US is riding the skid
built by a firm with the lowest bid." —*The Wordspinner*

Quality control is often as important in nature as it is in human industry. The female weaver bird selects her mate after surveying the nests her suitors have constructed. The best builder is then permitted to mate while the bachelors are cold shouldered back to the drawing board. One winning nest, I'm told, had interior lighting provided by fireflies fixed to the mud walls.

Thus, as the proverb states, it's the dweller not the architect that's the best judge of the *gestalt*. And since architectural critics often cannot afford to live in the homes of the people they are evaluating, they lack the perspective of the residents. Many owners of homes designed by Frank Lloyd Wright, for example, have complained of leaks, but individuals who feel freedom means being indifferent to quality never unrolled their Oriental carpets under a porous roof. In other words, the proof's in the pudding, not the recipe.

Though the infinity of *pi* is a perfect reflection of nature's imperfection, humans eventually stumbled on the Clovis design for a serviceable spear point. Starting about 13,500 BC, people across the New World used this basic design until copper, bronze, and iron points were developed. Today, the absence of technological change for even a year is rare. Since the Chinese introduced gunpowder in the ninth century, the rate at which weapons have changed has been exponential. Indeed, the restless search for better ways to kill is unceasing.

Yahweh touched tangentially on quality when He declared that Job was "perfect." That's the word the King James translators used, but later scribes felt that Job was merely a "good" man. A few generations later, Jehovah's son commanded people of quality to "perfect" themselves, but this was later revised to read make yourself "whole." Opinions, however, vary on what a perfect or a whole human would consist of if not divinely connected.

Across the Mediterranean, Muslims felt that any attempt to depict a human, plant, or animal blasphemed the perfection of Allah's creation. Verisimilitude, thus, became a sin because realistic artists appeared to be vying with God. To this day, carpets from the Orient have a deliberate defect woven into them as a sign of man's humility before his perfect creator. Thus, an antelope depicted with five legs is not only acceptable but "perfect."

While many Christians also had misgivings about making "graven images," the majority felt that the paintings of a Jan Van Eyck and "Bibles in stone" like the one at Chartres honored God. In 1992, the Roman Catholic Church conceded that "shoddy workmanship" was a sin. Yet at the same time, western capitalists were referring to "planned obsolescence" as a "healthy dissatisfaction," and "quality" was often preceded by "good."

The renewed appreciation of excellence which flowered in the Renaissance especially in the arts helped the West make up for the time lost to the East after the fall of Rome. Which is not to say that the East did not prize quality: the blades of Damascus, for example, were unsurpassed for five hundred years, but eventually western explosives spelled the scimitar's demise. Once the Spaniards had driven the

Moors off the Iberian Peninsula, they too lost sight of quality as they built their armada. One reason the Spanish lost that famed naval battle in the English Channel is that the cannon balls on one side of a ship did not fit the cannons on the other. Standardization is one way of insuring quality at a certain level, and as robots improve, they may replace the solitary watchmaker who spends years producing her masterwork.

Over the past hundred years or so, capitalism has developed a forked opinion of quality, which has led to the rise and fall of the ideal often within the same company. You might call it the "more-bricks-with-less-straw" vs. the "fewer-bricks-with-more-straw" debate. Without any cognitive dissonance, General Motors manufactured its well-made Cadillacs in one plant and their "unsafe at any speed" Corvairs in another. But no vehicle surpasses the Rolls-Royce in quality. Over half of all the Rolls ever built since 1906 are still on the highway. The rest, I suspect, are in museums, lacking only a fresh battery.

After WWII, the Federal Trade Commission, fearing Japanese camera makers would undermine the profits of Kodak, informed Nikon and others they could not export their wares to this country unless they met very high standards. Eventually Nikon met those standards, and Kodak, as we know, chose bankruptcy to adaptation. In the auto industry, the first postwar Japanese cars were considered by many to be laughably cheap. Fifty years later, Toyota occasionally beats GM in annual sales, while across the Pacific, GM products are often repainted before being placed in Japanese showrooms.

It's been observed that discussions of quality usually end on a mournful note: "Remember Aunt Essie's Pierce-Arrow—now that was a car." And because most quality merchandise like Hatteras yachts and Lexus automobiles are expensive, most discussions of it take place among the wealthy. That has not always been the case. My great grandfather Warren Alford built covered bridges in South Georgia that are still in use almost two hundred years after they were built. Once a flood knocked his bridge across Auchumpkee Creek off its foundations, but when the waters of the Flint River receded, the bridge was winched back into position. Yet the builder was not a wealthy aristocrat, nor does anyone mourn his bridges still in use.

My father, a veteran of WWII, brought home a single token of the war: a Zippo lighter issued by the Army. Until he quit smoking and threw away his lighter, it functioned perfectly. Dad liked to say that quantity, not quality, beat Hitler, and he had a point. Indeed, by the middle of 1945, Zippo lighters, jeeps, and B-29's were flying off American assembly lines so rapidly the Germans and Japanese did not stand a chance.

Still, I try to buy quality when I can afford it. Thus most of our "good" knives are Henckels, and most of my "good" tools are Craftsman. The reason is simple. If 99.9% is acceptable, nearly three hundred cardiac pacemaker operations will fail, over a hundred thousand income tax returns will be misfiled, and nearly twenty thousand prescriptions will be mis-labeled every year in this country alone.

※

The building in which my office once was located was completed in 1969. In 1989, a colleague entered his office one morning and discovered that a twelve-foot shelf and all its books had worked itself free of the wall and fallen across his desk. He was not injured in the collapse, but his coffee cup and printer were smashed. A carpenter from the university's physical plant came by a day later to reattach the shelf, and asked, "Do you want me to fix this temporarily or for twenty years?"

My colleague said, "The last guy to work on this put it up for twenty years, so I suggest you put it up forever or not at all." Just as "excellence is the best deterrent to racism or sexism," according to Oprah Winfrey, so is quality the best deterrent to the sky falling.

Can Anyone Afford to Stand Idly By? Questions

"It is [prideful] curiosity to enquire into that which God hath concealed." —*Samuel Hieron*

"[If your reporters had asked the right questions prior to the Bay of Pigs mission,] you would have saved us from a colossal mistake." —*John F. Kennedy speaking to a* New York Times *editor*

Here's a cautionary tale about a former student, Zoneeki Scott. (I've changed his name but not by much.) On the first day of class, I was reading the roll when I came to Scott's name, and I was so sure the computer had made a mistake, I said, "Scott Zoneeki?"

"Here, sir, but you have it backwards. My name is Zoneeki Scott."

"Your given name is Zoneeki?"

"Yes, sir."

"Interesting. I'm quite sure I've never heard your name before—how did you come by such an unusual name?"

"I don't know."

"You don't know?"

"No, sir—I don't know."

"Are there any uncles or grandfathers in your family named Zoneeki?"

"No, sir, not that I know of."

"Do you have any brothers or sisters?"

"Yes, sir."

"If you don't mind, what are their names?"

"William and Maryanne."

"William, Maryanne, and Zoneeki—and you never asked?"

"No, sir."

"What a shame. Be sure to ask next time you call home, OK?" And that was the end of it. Mr. Scott dropped the class shortly after the first quiz before he had a chance to satisfy my curiosity. Some might say "idle curiosity," but there was nothing idle about it, for in a sense, Zoneeki's life depended on it. I trust I shamed him into asking, but I'm not optimistic.

For years, when my humanities survey reached the Florentine Renaissance, I brought in a scaled-down industrial crane modeled on a design by Leonardo da Vinci. After pointing out a few clever design features, I placed it on a table near the door and said that if anyone had a question or just wanted to examine it to come by after class. No one ever stopped. Yet when I brought the same model to an Elder Hostel class, most wanted to operate it, and several had questions I could not answer. This, I told them, was good because it made all of us rethink Leonardo's blueprint and why he'd designed a crane strong enough to lift a small church in the first place.

Tom Thaves, the current author of *Frank and Ernest*, once asked with an implied wink whether the unanswered question or the unquestioned answer is worse. Since silence follows both, I'd say with a wink of my own that if the question is unanswerable, the answer will surely be unquestioned. Seriously though, for forty-two years as a teacher of literature I felt that no answer, especially in the texts we were examining, should be unquestioned, and I've never answered a student's question, even the rude and presumptuous, with silence. In fact, in many of my classes, a written question about the day's reading assignment was mandatory. One colleague has a requirement that every student ask or answer at least one question aloud in her classes. I tried that but could not abide the silence.

I've long believed in "doing for my brother," but I also believe in asking him first. I also feel that every question whether from a grandchild or a reporter deserves to be heard. Others say not every question deserves an answer, but how would you know what was undeserving until you've heard it? Realizing that no one knew him or his work as well as he did, Vladimir Nabokov required all questions from book reviewers to be submitted in advance. Then he choose the ones he felt were worthy of his attention and did not worry whether he would be misquoted. Reading Thoreau's statement that no one knew him as well as he did, James Dickey adopted a similar strategy when he wrote *Self-Interviews*. He made a list of good questions for himself and answered them in the comfort of his home speaking into a microphone. I did something of the sort after my parents died. I asked our son and daughter to send me ten questions they'd always wanted to ask before it was too late. Then over a few weeks, I answered in what became a twenty-page essay. Email makes this parental obligation all the easier.

When my father bought his first computer, the cat finally relaxed its grip on Dad's tongue especially in regard to the two wars he'd fought in. Over seven years, he answered dozens of questions that, when I was living at home, had usually been met with a shrug. I printed each of his emails, placed them in a binder, and they now represent the next best thing to having him at the end of this fiber-optic umbilical.

As I plotted how best to draw my father out, I realized that strategies for asking questions are as varied as answering. I've read that some reporters have taught themselves to take notes in their pockets so as not to intimidate their sources. I assume it helps to wear a cargo jacket. Studs Turkel used a contrary tactic as he fumbled with his tape recorder to help subjects feel self-confident. Other inquisitors like Howard Cosell and Mike Wallace have asked blunt or rude questions to provoke a subject. Truman Capote resorted to lying about his mother's attempts to seduce Cary Grant to lure the writer's subjects into an admission of their own indiscretions. I imagine we've all feigned ignorance at one time or another to see how our friends will fill in the blanks.

I am encouraged by ChaCha.com, the free, on-line search engine, which receives 600,000 questions daily, and which some human on the planet will answer in about three minutes. It's not face to face, but it gets those "fugitive and cloistered" questions answered.

Phillip Halsman often asked subjects to jump straight up from a squatting position in front of his camera. He then would photograph them at the point when and where their masks were farthest removed. Though there would be little time for a response at the apex of their leaps, that unguarded moment is when a question is best asked.

People jumping, when they are dressed to be photographed by one of the best in the business, can rarely keep a straight face, which brings me to the comic question: a genre developed by George Carlin and Steven Wright over the last thirty years. Typical of the genre is Wright's "What do you do when you see an endangered animal eating an endangered plant?" After a stunned moment, I answered my grandson, "I don't know—offer the poor beast a carrot?" Related to the comic question is the misnomer that's been twisted into a question such as, "What was King George VI's first name?" I fell for it and guessed "George";

it was "Albert." Nevertheless, I was pleased he asked me anything.

As a long-time public-radio listener and newscast viewer, I miss Tim Russert, late of NBC, and admire the work being done by Fareed Zakaria on CNN. But I've seen and heard dozens of interviews, parts of which have irritated me. Chief among the irritants is the host who invites several notable guests and permits them to talk over each other. The result, of course, is mere noise. Then there's the host who interrupts guests in mid-sentence or talks almost as much as they do. There's also the type who with thirty seconds left asks, "So, Herr Hitler, what have you been doing in Argentina since the war?" Finally, there's the type who thinks his all-declarative speech contains an interrogative. More than once, I've found myself saying to the radio, "Is there a question in there?"

Will Rogers said he'd rather be the man who bought the Brooklyn Bridge than the one who sold it—naïve, that is, rather than scheming. Likewise, if my choices were limited, I'd rather be the lamb-like interviewee than the wolfish interviewer. But in reality, I would be neither. I've always wanted my children and students to ask questions like good reporters—who, what, when, where, why, and how—so they will never be in the position of *Pravda's* subscribers reading their newspaper's apology for fifty years of lies.

No one has conducted an interview with more aplomb than Walter Cronkite, "the most trusted man in America," late of CBS News. In 1977, he asked such challenging and provocative questions of Anwar El-Sadat that the Egyptian President volunteered to meet with Israel's Prime Minister Menachem Begin. The following day, he was invited to Jerusalem, and before long, the Camp David Accords were signed. It all began with some hard but respectful questions.

Curled Up by Love: Reading to Children

"Dear Madam: Will you please let this nigger boy have some books by H. L. Mencken?" —Note forged by Richard Wright

*"Thanks to my books for their incandescence
that saved me from my adolescence." —The Wordspinner*

Judging from the pictures, I was about five when my grandfather said that his idol Rogers Hornsby had never read a book, and that was the main reason he hit .358 over twenty-three years in the majors. Apparently my father didn't think much of his father's eye-strain argument because I have two photographs of him reading the Sunday comics to me on the porch of my grandfather's home.

I was fortunate that my parents read to me before I could read for myself, so I have forwarded their gift into the foggy future by reading to our children and grandchildren. I'm happy to report that my efforts and the work of several others appear to be bearing fruit: three of our grandchildren are fine readers, and the youngest soon will be. I always expected that our daughter and daughter-in-law would read to their children, but our son and son-in-law also appreciate that there is no cheaper or wiser investment.

The male stereotype, judging mostly by *New Yorker* cartoons over the last forty years, is for the father, if he reads at all to his children, to be a reluctant reader. In one cartoon, a father watching television tells his pajama-clad daughter holding a book, "A story? Honey, wouldn't you rather a mild sedative?" Another child sitting in bed finds it necessary to remind his father that reading a story requires reading *aloud*. One rare patriarch actually shoulders his responsibility and reads "Billy Pig's Picnic" to an unseen child. Standing in a corner of a book store, this father reads into his cell phone. Though it's a novel form of piracy, I suppose that "distance learning" beats no story at all.

The children in these bedtime cartoons are an alien breed. One budding gangster tells his grandmother seated beside the bed with a book in her hand, "I'll listen for a dollar." Another kid raises the ante telling his father, "Mommy usually reads me a story, then slips me a twenty." Often the child is a confederate of the mother as when one girl whispers past her father, whose book has slipped to the floor, "I think he's finally asleep." One thing is certain: children are more comfortable with the technology than their elders. In one panel, a child is happily listening to "Peter Pan" on her iPod while her grandfather reads the *Times*.

I realize that cartoons aren't a blood-pressure cuff on the arm of civilization, but I also know how hard many have fought for the right to read whatever they wish. In my lifetime, it once was against South Carolina state law for the Pickens County Bookmobile to stop in black neighborhoods. In the same county where John C. Calhoun once blustered, "Show me a nigger who can ... parse a Greek verb, and I'll admit he's a human being," the bookmobile wouldn't even slow down. Just a county away, Jesse Jackson was denied entrance to the Greenville County Public Library when he was a high-school senior working on a term paper. And a few counties to the east, future astronaut Ronald McNair was forbidden to use a library that his African-American family had helped to build with their tax dollars.

In 2008, the novelist Dave Eggers told a Clemson audience about orphans in Ethiopia being taught to read and write in a boys' "school" without desks, books, paper, or pencils. The students, when they write at all, write in the dirt with an index finger. If their letters are not well formed, their teacher often pushes their "pen" into the clay so hard the nails crack. A few Clemson athletes were in the audience the night Eggers spoke, and I hope they understood his message. I mention them because many enjoy full scholarships, and yet they often resell their texts with the shrink-wrap unbroken. But isn't having books you never read like leaving all the lights on while you sleep?

A colleague of mine was in the USC-Sumter Registrar's Office a few years ago, when a young black man brought an application for graduate school to the counter. After a few questions, it was clear that the sheepish applicant could neither read nor write. The Sumter registrar then called his counterpart at Morris College and asked if the applicant was one of their graduates as he'd claimed. "Oh, yes," the Morris administrator assured him after checking the records, "he was one of our non-reading graduates." I have several responses to this disturbing tale, but I shall leave it at this: it's likely this poor fellow was a victim of a family that never read to him.

Unfortunately, not every child has a mother like the pediatric neurosurgeon, Dr. Benjamin Carson. Although Carson's mother was illiterate, she insisted her son read to her every day because she understood the importance of what she'd been denied, namely that:

The sword's in a book, not buried in stone.
Until it is freed, you can't take the throne.

In another crotchet of mine called "The Shape of Love,"

I write:

A man with a small girl reading "one more story"
is a sunflower curled by a morning glory.

A parent who cannot afford fifteen minutes a day to be curled by the demands of his child is a man too busy to be a father. If parents spend any time at home, they have time to tell a story even if they cannot read one. There's just no excuse. Don't have a story? Then borrow one of mine: Once upon a time, Mrs. Henny Penny went to a library and said to the librarian, "Buk!" After presenting her library card, the hen left with her book properly stamped. The next day, she returned and said, "Buk, buk!" Soon, Mrs. Penny checked out with two books and returned the following day, saying, "Buk, buk, buk!" Curious, the librarian followed the hen home. "Can she really read two books," he wondered, "in a day?" Standing at the open window of the hen's coop, he saw her place each of the books before a frog. To her adopted offspring, she said, "Read it, read it, read it!"

And that is how the frog came to speech.

Take it from Mrs. Penny; she knows a thing or two: the frog grew up to be a neurosurgeon.

Alien Sex and the Green Revolution: Research

"A footnote more seductive than the text
is a catnap that's better than sex." — *The Wordspinner*

"Research is what I'm doing when I don't know what I'm doing."
— *Wernher von Braun*

If by any chance you're not a regular reader of the *Nathaniel Hawthorne Newsletter*, *American Speech*, or the *Hemingway/Fitzgerald Journal*, let me introduce myself. I once helped to edit the first of these academic journals; I elaborated on the origins of "redneck" in the second, and I revealed that Scott Fitzgerald had blundered in the third. And they say *Gatsby* is the perfect novel; I guess I settled that.

One would think my editorial stint alone would have earned me a Wiki page, but if I have one, I cannot find it. Truth is, after six years of reading essays by Hawthorne scholars and graduate students hungry for a publication, I felt that if I ever saw another note or query on *The Scarlet Letter* it would be too soon.

My ground-breaking work in *American Speech* did earn me a sentence on the Wiki page devoted to "redneck." Yes, there is one, and I found it. Along with a few other discoveries, it earned me a promotion. Five years of graduate work living much of it on government cheese had finally paid off.

In graduate school, when I discovered that the Duke of Buccleuch (a possible relative of Nick's) and the Earl of Doncaster (Gatsby's Oxford classmate) were one and the same, Dr. Bruccoli, my professor said, "My boy, you've got the makings of a real scholar." Then he reached in his pocket and pulled out a duplicate of the medal King Nicolas of Montenegro presented Gatsby after WWI. According to Fitzgerald, the medal's reverse side reads, "Major Jay Gatsby, For Valour Extraordinary." I swear Bruccoli had the thing in his pocket. At any rate, we both realized that the ceramic-coated medal had no place for any inscription at all. Fitzgerald had stumbled again. Bruccoli then flattered me saying he wanted to publish my insights in the *Hemingway/Fitzgerald Journal,* which he'd founded and was still editing. It was my first publication outside of a few poems published in equally obscure journals.

I have reams of work establishing the location of Browning's inspiration for "The Bishop Orders His Tomb," the guilt of Poe's narrator in "Ulalume" who is returning to the scene of his crime, and the refusal of Morgan Robertson to capitalize on the similarities between his novel *Futility* and the Titanic's sinking fourteen years later. Though I read all of this research at various small conferences, no one would publish it, or I might have been made an alumni professor and taken from the classroom altogether.

❄

Of course, my tongue is deep in my cheek in the paragraphs above, but I confess I played the publication game for forty years despite what I'd realized as an undergraduate: the worst classroom teachers are often the most prolific publishers. I had one pedant, highly regarded by his pedantic peers, who came to a graduate class in modern drama and read the assigned plays to us. When we reached Edward Albee, I thought, "Finally—I know he's been working on an Albee monograph; perhaps now we can discuss the plays we've read." But I was disappointed again when he read to us from his manuscript.

Dr. James Barker, the former president of the school where I once taught, told his faculty, "Research is, in fact, the engine that drives the quality of teaching at a university." That may be true for graduate classes in physics or engineering, but except for a few rare exceptions, it isn't for most undergraduate classes in the humanities or even introductory calculus. How far do you think that redneck-pellagra connection took me in my history of the language classes?

During the 2007-2008 recession that hit my former department very hard, I volunteered to teach one class of thirty-five without pay. As I reminded the new chair, I was comfortably retired and simply wanted to serve. Though my suggestion stood to make the department over $30,000 per semester, I was turned down because "teaching without pay would set a bad precedent." I said I'd teach a class for a dollar. The chair smiled and said, "I'll pay you $6,000 whether you need it or not." So, I did this for six semesters and pocketed $36,000, which might have gone to reduce the departmental deficit.

When I suggested cutting back on the departmental research expectations and asking full professors to teach freshman English, or nine hours instead of six per week, I was spurned again. In 2008, I read that 102 Shakespearian monographs had been published the previous year while tuition and student debt continued to climb.

❊

Research, which Zora Neale Hurston called "formalized curiosity ... poking and prying with a purpose," has a motleyed history. Relaxing in his recliner, Aristotle, scoured his brain and "discovered" that swallows don't migrate; they hibernate in the same fertile mud that produces eels. His "research" also revealed that thrown objects travel in a straight path, never curved; tigers have a spike at the end of their tail, and female adults have fewer teeth than men. For over a thousand years "doing research" meant "checking to see what Aristotle had said."

Deep into the middle ages, while some scholastic philosophers were debating the number of teeth a horse had (apparently no one had an Aristotelian text to check), a student dashed outside and counted a horse's teeth or so the probably apocryphal story goes. At that point, however, whether it was teeth or rose petals, modern science was born. For science, or "knowledge" as the Greeks called it, absolutely depends on the very close scrutiny of nature. Peer review, multiple witnessing, and double-blind testing would come later, but Aristotle's influence would last well into the nineteenth century.

Counting your wife's or your horse's teeth may sound absurd, but it is the foundation of all scientific research. But before the counting begins, there's often a fantasy. As a boy, Einstein tried to imagine himself on a carpet flying at light speed with a flashlight in his hand. "Would the flashlight illuminate the way ahead?" he wondered. This speculation ultimately led to his theory of relativity. This then led others to test the theory which led to atomic clocks, which are capable of some very accurate measurements. These then led to the GPS system that many now use to navigate instead of maps. Like the fifteenth-century maps with dragons along the margins, the GPS system offers endless ways to reach and perhaps slay the dragons of modernity.

When a friend in the humanities was designated a "master teacher," his reward was a salary bump and a three-hour reduction in classroom time. Despite the respectful designation, the dean really wanted him to do more research.

Academic job applicants are rarely asked to teach a class before the search committee; instead, they are asked to read some of their research. The result of this emphasis especially at the undergraduate level, has led to the current situation where there are seven journals devoted to James Joyce; half of all scientific research is never cited by another author, and hundreds of articles are withdrawn annually because of error or fraud. Too much of what is allowed to stand, is poop-in-a-pot or porcupine work: "If drug X has Y effect on rats and mice, let's see what effect it has on porcupines."

Research in the humanities is another kettle of corn. As one scientist in a penny-ante poker game said, "I'll see your Hawthorne article and raise you the iPhone." That's a pricy and dicey bet in any case, but I suspect the over-confident scientist doesn't understand the ultimate goal of humanistic research. In part, it's about exposing Fitzgerald's errors, but ultimately it's about helping readers and the researcher understand the bond they share with every human from Sarawak to Schenectady. To be sure, the iPhone has made it easier to contact Malaysians, but the humanist gives us a reason to contact them as well as something to say.

I Think; Therefore, Iamb: Rhythm and Rime

"The rhythm we learned rolling in the womb
is a beat unlearned only in the tomb." —*The Wordspinner*

"It is no small joy watching Ferlingetti
hunting rime on the Serengeti." —*The Wordspinner*

Wystan Hugh Auden claimed that "poetry makes nothing happen," and William Carlos Williams claimed that it contains information which, when absent, people die from. So which is it? After reading of Dr. Alain Bombard's brave experiment in which he drifted across the Atlantic with the trade winds but without food or water, I figured Dr. Williams had the upper hand. So I thought if I could versify what Bombard learned on his voyage, I could achieve immortality and save lives in short order. And so I have written:

One may survive
a wreck at sea
if one starts to drink
immediately
a pint of brine
per day for thirst
and a squirt of plankton
seined in a shirt.
I wanted to write this
that along the way
a poem may be said
to have saved the day.

Perhaps this is immodest of me, but if these verses have any legs, it's not so much my substance as the style, the rhythm and rime, which will propel them into the future.

Song writers, like poets, have a license to lie, but no one should monkey-wrench with the melody. Anyone who's spent a spring in Paris knows the weather in May is usually warmer and drier than April, but the trochaic rhythm of Yip Harburg's line "April in Paris" demanded a lie in 1932 when it was written. And despite climate change, it still demands it. In the tribute to Dr. Bombard above, I might have written "a quart of brine," but shipwreck survivors might have died if they'd followed my advice. However, if the meter had required "liter of brine," I might have given in to the temptation, for such is the power of rhythm over life. As every Catholic knows, children are born when that lunar rhythm is ignored.

Planned or unplanned, children who are losing weight will often nurse better and cry less when a recording of the mother's heartbeat is piped into the nursery. Increase or decrease the tempo of those familiar iambs, and the child will become agitated again. When tests showed that a friend was infertile, her sister volunteered to be a surrogate. One of her eggs was then fertilized by the husband of the first and implanted in the womb of the second. You should know that the second woman was a swimmer who swam almost daily through her pregnancy. So after the baby was born and was reluctant to nurse, the lactation specialist urged the second, who was fit, just not fit-fit, to lower her heart rate via exercise, and soon the baby was nursing contentedly. It was all in the rhythm as any baseball pitcher can tell you.

Brain scans of infants just a few hours old prove not only that babies recognize their mothers' voices but the natural rhythms of their mother's language. Moreover, French babies will almost always turn toward an unfamiliar French speaker who is reading a list of two-syllable words. The reason for the turn is that French is very regular in stressing the second syllable. German babies, on the other hand, will turn toward a German speaker because two-syllable words in German typically receive an accent on the first syllable.

Malcolm Usrey, a former colleague, argued that nursery rimes were "Neolithic paregoric." Moreover, he said, human speech may have originated in Paleolithic caves when mothers made rhythmic sounds to lull their babies to sleep or coax young wolves into the caves as they began the process of domestication. It would be a long time, however, before Milton's angels would soar.

As has often been noted, just because two words rime doesn't mean they belong together. In Neil Diamond's hit "Play Me," the narrator sings, "Song she sang to me / song she brang to me..." on the assumption that the verb "to bring" is as irregular as "to sing." It isn't. The first time I heard Diamond's song, I revoked his poetic license. It's a right every listener and reader possesses.

Though they have much in common, poetry and song have long competed for listeners. It's fair to say no poet has ever earned as much money as Stephen Sondheim or Oscar Hammerstein, yet few of their song lyrics are as artfully written as William Butler Yeats's "The Lake Isle of Innisfree." The irony of this particular choice is that Yeats was so tone deaf, he often did not recognize the Irish national anthem when he heard it. According to his son and daughter-in-law, Yeats's tin ear could not distinguish between a fiddle and a flute, but there's no denying that their ancestor got the job done. We just don't know how he did it. My guess is that his peerless vision compensated for the failure of his ears.

Despite the competition alluded to above, Ezra Pound thought "the poem fails when it strays too far from song…." I think most poets recognize that, but engineers and mathematicians may struggle with the concept. In 1842, Charles Babbage, who in Emily Dickinson's words had the "facts" of the world's rising population "without the phosphorescence," felt so strongly about "The Vision of Sin" by Alfred Lord Tennyson that he urged the poet to recast, "Every minute dies a man / Every minute one is born." Babbage, the father of the computer, thought the following would be preferable, "Every moment dies a man / Every moment one and a sixteenth is born." I understand Babbage's concern for accuracy, and "moment" is appropriately less precise than "minute," but no suspension bridge need fear his meter.

The origins of meter and rime are lost in prehistory which is surely where they were first used as mnemonic and organizing devices before writing was introduced. Genghis Khan reportedly had his orders transcribed into rhyming couplets for the benefit of the illiterate hordes who were doing his bidding. In the thirteenth century, a Benedictine monk rimed 137 rules of business math to help his fellows remember them. Shakespeare thought a pretty rime might win a lady's favor, but today if rime is not used to pique the memory ("Click it, or ticket"), we employ it lightly it for its pleasure: "Shake and shake / The catsup bottle. / None will come / And then a lot'll" (Richard Armour).

In that spirit, Robert Lowell wrote Elizabeth Bishop that rime and meter are "intoxicating," as indeed they are. Oddly, however, he felt that "they have nothing at all to do with the truth…." And, as rime and meter have nothing to do with the truth of the poet's experience, he said, so too are ballet steps irrelevant to the hiker. But as Rudolf Nureyev did a *grand jeté* to escape his KGB guards while he was "hiking" at a Paris airport, so too does the truth of Richard Armour's observation depend in part on managing the rhythm and rime. To see and hear my point, change Armour's "a lot'll" to, "a great deal will issue from the container." As should be apparent, the soufflé has fallen.

❋

Contrary to what my title above implies, I'm a trochee. Given that "Sterling Kenwood Eisiminger, Junior," my full given name, is trochaic pentameter, how could I feel any differently in an iambic English world? In my fifth decade of writing riming verse with little success, could it be that this falling rhythm is a sign I'm on the skids? "No way," Skip said spondaically.

An Improbable Fiction for Lena: The Language of Shakespeare

"If your native tongue is inadequate to the task, hijack another's."
—The Wordspinner

It's an improbable fiction to be sure dating to about 1575, but thereby hangs a youthful tale by Willie Snackspoor.

"Soft, my child. The post brings sad tidings that my once joyful mother is sicklied o'er with the pale cast of thought. Holp me if it please thee, for I have laundry to pound on Avon's stony banks. For the nonce, bear this claret and these sweetmeats to our ailing kinswoman.

"I fain would bring myself thither, Mother, come what may, for you alone have taught me to make a virtue of necessity. Sweet *are* the uses of adversity, but our moon-calf father is not one of them."

"Marry, young Russet. Now, don thy hooded cape incarnadine and hie thee to the forest o'er yon high eastward hill. Keep to the path no matter how the harebells beckon, and, I beseech you, beware the fantasied forest. There a wolf named Lupus dwells, swift as a shadow, and thus beggars all other description. Verily, he must be eschewed, for he will surely cozen you. Should you perchance to meet the rascal, screw thy courage to the sticking place, and hasten to thy destination."

Under a fair welkin, Russet sallied into great Birnam Wood buoyed by the milk of human kindness and determined to keep her spotless reputation, but something other than an exaltation of larks was on the wind....

"Whence cometh thou, cousin? Whose foot, albeit a

pretty one, is this that doth bestride my demesne?" saith a voice betwixt two gnarled oaks.

"But Birnam Wood belongs unto our liege lord, sirrah. Lo where he cometh!"

"Thou art an impudent lass. Our lord is making a weary pilgrimage to Canterbury. Tell me, I prithee, where art thou bound?"

"Avaunt, sirrah! If you must know, I go to my grandam's cottage famed for its gingerbread."

"Gramercy, thou saucy maid. Dally awhile picking herbs and primroses in yonder glade for your Grandam. Your dun basket lacks both health and color."

Off Lupus hied to the cottage where the smell of hot ginger had once wafted from the oven. Betwixt the shadows, Russet heard, "What fools these mortals be," but she could not comprehend the source.

"Good morrow, Grandam," saith the wolf and swallowed her alive as she screamed, "Fie! Prodigious birth, what is this beast upon my doorstep?" The poor woman had scarcely a chance to protest too much. Anon, after donning the mistress's bedfrock to clothe his naked villainy, he heard a knock at the door.

"'Zounds, my dear, thy comely virtues art most delicious whilst I myself have seen better days."

"I prithee, though thy voice is uncommon, Grandam, vouchsafe me a word with thee," saith Russet. But under her breath she muttered, "Jesus bless us, chaos is come again!"

Her senses returning, Russet inquired, "What change, Grandam, hath come to thy beauteous face?"

"Life's fitful fever, my sweet—my salad days withered years ago."

"But, Grandam, wherefore is thy rheumy eye so large?"

"The better to see thee with, my dear."

But wherefore is thy nose so long and hairy?"

"The better to smell thee with, my dear."

"But wherefore art thy teeth sharper than a serpent's?"

"The better to eat you with," saith the valiant trencherman, who sprang from the bed and devoured the virgin of spotless reputation. Sated at last, he undressed being disposed to sleep. His harsh snoring, however, attracted a humble swain passing beyond the cottage.

When he saw the strange bedfellow, he shouted in at the open door, "What the dickens? It smells to heaven in here! Murther will out, thou gorbellied, clapper-clawing knave!" Drawing his bodkin and slashing the pudding of the wolf's belly, our unsung bachelor released Grandam and Russet, slimy but unharmed, from their warm constraint like newborn twins a-tumble. In the gaping hollow, the swain placed an unswept stone and stitched up the wound. On waking, Lupus was so thirsty he did run to a village cesspool, and leapt headlong therein. Descending for the third time, he was heard to say, "Beshrew me, but methinks the game is up—a plague upon your houses! Farewell to all my greatness!"

In the great thorny wood, a parliament of owls hooted their approval.

After bathing, Grandam, whose odd humor had passed, set the table, and the three dined merrily on the contents of Russet's fardel and the last of the Yuletide ginger. By my troth, the world was their oyster at last.

Slipping in and out of Eden: Romances

"If you believe in your dreams, you run the risk of spending your entire life asleep."—*Chinese proverb*

"The ability to delude yourself is an important survival tool." — *Jane Wagner*

The history of antebellum South Carolina is replete with stories of dashing cavalrymen and hoop-skirted women who vow to wait till hell freezes over. The initial phase of romance is what Anita Brookner called "that wonderful beginning" since the middle and end are anyone's guess. The middle for Charleston began in the winter 1863 when the frozen city faced the flames of its endgame. This complex romantic saga is neatly encapsulated in the story of Lt. George Dixon and his sweetheart, Queenie Bennett. When the war began, Queenie gave her betrothed a newly minted, twenty-dollar gold piece with an embossed portrait of Miss Liberty resembling Queenie, or so Dixon thought. At Shiloh, a Union bullet hit the coin in Dixon's pocket and ricocheted away. As soon as he recovered from the bruising, Dixon had the reverse side of his coin sanded and engraved, "Shiloh/April 6, 1862/My life Preserver/GD." Less than two years later, Dixon drowned minutes after sinking the USS Housatonic. The CSS Hunley, piloted by Dixon, had accomplished the first successful destruction of an enemy vessel by a submarine. In 2001, Dixon's remains and Bennett's coin were recovered from the rusting hulk of the ship that took Queenie's beau to the bottom of Charleston harbor.

"Bless their hearts," as many South Carolinians might

say of Dixon and Bennett, but I grew up in a feet-on-the-ground family that subscribed to a newspaper, *Time*, *National Geographic*, and several others of a similar ilk. I cannot recall my mother watching a soap opera or my father escaping into fiction. The only exception was the time Dad injured his leg in jump school at Ft. Benning. Someone brought him Thomas Costain's *Below the Salt*, a footstool-sized historical romance, and he surprised everyone by finishing it. But as soon as he was off the footstool and on his feet again, it was back to magazines like *The Military Engineer*.

When my father found himself without a war to fight in Germany, he promptly volunteered for the invasion of Japan. When that "theater of operations" resolved itself while he was sailing toward the Pacific, he came home, warless. However, he soon found himself in Korea, and I don't recall that he regretted the transfer. To Dad, wars were not glorious, flag-waving adventures; instead, they were opportunities to be promoted.

Knowing what I know of my father's raising, I should not blame him for the failure of his romantic imagination. When our family went to visit our paternal grandparents in 1957, my younger sister, who was nine at the time, asked Dad if he would stop the car about half a block short of his old home. While I watched from the backseat, she ran to the door with a hat pulled down to her eyes, knocked on the door, and asked the lady of the house, "Would you like to buy some Girl Scout cookies?" Said her grandmother, who had not seen her in several years, "I know you're Karen. I saw your father stop down the street. Now take off that silly hat and come inside." Over fifty years later, my sister says she still remembers the keen disappointment when Grandmother Eisiminger refused to indulge her.

Perhaps this incident and my parents' influence in a roundabout way helps to explain why I prefer reading nonfiction though I have written poetry for forty years. As my wife of the same period claims, "Skip would rather carry a box of tampons to work than a Harlequin Romance." She's right, but I have not always been that way. As an adolescent, I reminded myself of Henry Fleming in *The Red Badge of Courage*. This was largely due to my obsession with the *Victory at Sea* television series about the naval battles of the Atlantic and Pacific in World War II, not Henry's tales of medieval chivalry. When I went to the firing range in basic training, the closest thing to a hot war I experienced, I wondered where the resonant voice-over and Richard Rogers' music were.

There's an old story about a woman who wheels her granddaughter into a photographer's studio. The elderly female clerk says, "Oh, what an adorable little face!" Says the grandmother, "Wait till you see her pictures." Realist that I am, I don't embrace photographs, but I usually indulge the fantasies of those who do. Sometimes, however, the temptation to re-anchor the feet of those I love is overwhelming. When our children were growing up, I was the parent who pointed out that Jack may have run up the hill to fetch a pail of water, but there's little likelihood of a well on a hilltop when wells were dug by hand. Moreover, I was pleased when our daughter compensated for the loss of her father with an imaginary friend while I was absent in graduate school. But I was even more pleased when Ookpick disappeared on the heels of my return. Yes, I was jealous of a fictional surrogate.

Vibrating near the leading edges of my frontal lobes is the memory of my first landlady, a widow of many years. I did not know her before her husband died, but like

Margaret Mitchell, author of *Gone with the Wind*, Carrie was apparently compensating for what life had neglected to provide her. She lived in a world with no PMS, acne, or colonoscopies but with lots of amnesia, sudden paralysis, and temporary blindness. In her world, all the firewood was cut, split, and stacked in the basement, or as one kindling dealer put it in his newspaper ad, "all the romance without the heartache." In her world, Tuscany was good, South Dakota was bad; castle towers were white, silos were black; and *yin* never mixed with *yang*. I'll never forget how crushed Carrie was when CBS's *Dallas* came to an end and Bobby Ewing revealed that the entire fourteen-season run had been a dream.

Having said all that, I must admit that my wife and I once were fans of ABC's *Desperate Housewives*. We did not miss an episode in six seasons, and regardless of what concert was on PBS or what football game was on NBC, every Sunday we took a trip down Wisteria Lane to watch "the wives." Like Shakespeare's "penny stinkards," we cheered and booed as our favorites rose and fell. It was all great fun. Our friends and family thought that cups were missing from our cupboard, but we never felt a need to justify how we furnished our kitchen. We were not exhibiting the romantic folly of the Polish cavalry when the *Wehrmacht* came calling in tanks; we were just slipping back into the Garden of Eden for an hour. We resumed our responsibilities at ten.

Averting the Snide Effects: Satire

"Religions, like all other ideas, deserve criticism, satire, and, yes, our fearless disrespect." —*Salman Rushdie*

"A discriminating irreverence is the creator and protector of human liberty." —*Mark Twain*

In 1989, "Steve," I'll call him, discovered a photograph taken when he was a boy of about thirteen. It was noteworthy because the picture had been made by the WPA photographer and Pulitzer-Prize-winning writer Eudora Welty. Standing on a boxcar in a Mississippi rail yard, Steve was dressed in a suit while several others were dressed in more casual attire. All were staring intently at something unknown beyond the picture frame. Despite the informality of the setting, the triangular composition reminded some of pedimental sculpture. Indeed, "monumentally stiff" is a phrase many would still use to describe Steve, a recognized scholar who smote many as self-important. When a former colleague returned to Steve's school and heard that he was still living, she said, "I thought he would have died of concern."

For days, Steve carried Welty's volume of photographs with him in his briefcase. Spotting the unwary, he would sometimes intrude on a conversation to show them his picture. Some began avoiding the college's second-floor lounge just because Steve might be lurking.

One day, on the departmental bulletin board, another photograph, *circa*. 1940, appeared. This one showed a young man in a suit eagerly greeting a Good Humor man. Typed at the bottom was the caption: "Another old photograph of Steve." He soon got the message.

Some twenty-five years later, long after Steve had died, I found the notes I'd taken in 1989 in my satire file, typed them up, and sent them to several former colleagues. One, who was much closer to Steve than I had been, was not amused, and wrote, "Skip, I'm not sure I like that story. I may not understand it, but it strikes me as petty."

I was stung, but I replied, "…as the messenger in this story, I apologize if I hurt your feelings. Of course, many still feel that while Steve could be a good colleague, he was often the sand in the departmental oyster. You may recall that he asked one new hire, 'Why did you go to Wake Forest [an inferior school in Steve's view] for your B. A.? There's no one there.' The captioned but unsigned picture, however, that appeared on the bulletin board effectively lubricated the irritant. All in all, it's a good example of how satire should work—namely, by not descending into libel or slander. Thus, the stray oyster is brought back into the fold. As Jonathan Swift said, 'My satire's not for my target's approval but for his reform.' Though in the process of reforming, the satirist may appear self-righteous and even petty, as you say, the target *was* reformed…."

It should come as no surprise that people are hurt when they take joking matters too seriously. My friend Kurt Schneider, who flew for the Luftwaffe in WWII, illustrated this for me just a few weeks before he died. For reasons no doctor ever explained or perhaps understood, Kurt was congenitally susceptible to jaundice and was sent on multiple occasions to the infirmary where he lay for a few days before being ordered back to the front. During one hospital stay near the war's end, some of his friends paid him a visit, and in a solemn but ironic ceremony, they presented him with an Iron Cross, crudely cut from a tin can. A short while later, and despite Kurt's obvious symptoms, an SS officer also paid Kurt a visit to investigate the rumor of his malingering. A nurse assured the officer he wasn't, which so angered him, he tried ripping the decoration from Kurt's neck. The string, however, was stronger than he reckoned, and he shredded his hand in the attempt. Off he went to have it sewn up, and fortunately Kurt never saw him or combat again.

My mentor James Dickey, a master of the verbal razor himself, told students that the best satire severs an ear from the body so deftly with one hand, it leaves the appendage in place while offering bandages with the other. When Joan Rivers called Michelle Obama a "tranny" (a transgendered individual) on CNN, she was not satirizing the First Lady, just slandering her. Raw defamation like Hitler's use of "vermin" for Jews implies no corrective issuing as it does from the reptilian core.

One of the best examples of the satirical style I favor was a sign held up for television cameras at the 1974 Oscars. The neatly lettered sign urged members of the Academy to honor Richard Nixon with the prize for "best editing of a sound recording." Deserving as he was, the disgraced president didn't win, but he did resign. The same year, Gary Trudeau won a Pulitzer Prize for his strip showing a massive brick wall going up around the White House. To fully appreciate the strip, one must know that Nixon popularized the infinitive "to stonewall." Given the later confessions of Nixon and Bill Clinton, I'd say the satires above were effective, for the implied correctives were adopted.

Dickey's description, however, while useful, skirts the issue of limits. To satirists like Salman Rushdie, quoted at the top of this essay, whether they use brickbats or razors, there are few if any limits. The more discriminating Mark

213

Twain, however, also quoted above, hints at the dangers of roasting over an open flame.

Over several years, eleven cartoonists, writers, and editors at *Charlie Hebdo*, a French satirical magazine, taunted Islam so they could, as one editor put it, "die standing [rather] than living on [their] knees." On January 7, 2015, they were murdered by two angry Muslims. These eleven had been duly warned about the dangers of "standing" by hundreds of Muslims, Christians, Jews, and the French police, for *any* visual representation of Allah or Mohammed is considered idolatry and worthy of punishment. *Charlie* not only published images of Mohammed, he pictured him naked and bent over. Among the twenty dead that tragic day in Paris were four French-Jewish citizens and two gendarmes. By my accounting, some of the blame for those six deaths must be attributed to *Charlie Hebdo's* insistence on "standing." It would not have hurt to bend the knee.

Marching under the banner "Nothing Is Sacred," of course, invites an attack from those who find much that is sacred. *Charlie Hebdo's* editor Stéphane Charbonnier boasted that after decades of satirizing Roman Catholicism he could now "show the pope sodomizing a mole and get no reaction" because the banalization of Catholicism was complete. As parents who have survived their children's adolescence know, the immature love to pull the tail of a horse's ass. Rarely, however, is the horse reformed, and often it will kick.

Unless I'm discussing *Huckleberry Finn*, I have no reason to use the n- word. My black fellows may use it but should not. The line for either race, however, is difficult to define. To help, I suggest the "Three-Voter Test": if two of three reasonable people randomly chosen find something offensive, rethink it. Like child pornography, hate speech is an exception to America's cherished freedoms, and the rights of one should not intrude on the rights of another.

※

Moliere made his name on the French stage in part by satirizing the church and the medical profession. Much of the criticism was deserved given the many pedophiles and quacks lurking under the collar and cloak of respectability. On February 17, 1673, however, Moliere and his cast may have expected too much from their target audience. While acting in the title role of *The Imaginary Invalid*, the tubercular playwright collapsed on stage. When the call went out for a doctor in the house, no one came. When last rites were requested, no priest answered the call.

As his son, I'd defend Moliere's right to use satire, but as his father, I'd warn him of its dangers.

The Sound of Mucus: Sentiment and Sentimentality

"Tears are a liquor Louise loves to slop
as Lucky loves the swill from her mop." — *The Wordspinner*

"Jack plowed a straight furrow and seldom looked back,
though his rye tended to shrug off the slack." — *The Wordspinner*

Recently, I attended an OLLI lecture in which a pediatric surgeon recalled forty years in the OR. As he spoke, he flashed through a dozen slides of some unconscious children he'd operated on for everything from swallowed toys to brain tumors. But he spoke of these surgeries as dispassionately as if he'd been pulling stumps from a burned-over pasture. Though the children's faces had been blurred, I often found myself choking up thinking about what his patients had endured. When the unmoved speaker was through, I asked him how he'd steadied his hands and dried his eyes in his efforts to help the children. He said that it was a long learning process aided by a professional staff hardened to suffering and a laser-like focus on the work at hand.

"I don't mean any offense," I said, "but didn't this process turn you into something of a robot?"

"In some ways, I suppose it did," he said smiling, "but I'm a machine who cannot kill a mouse."

When I told my wife of this exchange, she reminded me of the time in Columbus when she'd had a seizure at the bank where she worked. A colleague had taken her to the hospital which is where I found her when I returned from Auburn, about thirty miles away. The next morning, while she was being prepped for an angiogram, Dr. "Kalter Fisch," as we came to call him, breezed in as he made his rounds with an entourage of sleepy interns. Without saying anything to my wife of a personal or consoling nature during his tour, he turned to leave, saying over his shoulder, "Of course, this patient may have a brain tumor." My wife and I were stunned, for this was the first mention of such a thing though it had ricocheted around my skull the night before. Though the scan showed no tumor, and a prescription brought the seizures under control, "Kalter Fisch" still strikes me as a machine who could kill a mouse.

Now it's true, my wife *might* have had a tumor, and the interns *should* have been reminded of the possibility, but why couldn't the doctor's heartless speculation have been disseminated beyond our reach? I'm reminded of Jon Moulton, the British venture capitalist, who lists "insensitivity" as one of his "three most valuable character traits." Apparently, sentiment just gets in the way of those who liquidate "lives" with no more of an apology than, "Watch my dust!"

At some point, these three men were fitted with "heart clamps" which stunted the fullness of their growth, though some less severely than others as illustrated by the pediatric surgeon above. They are not alone, of course, for appeals to animal lovers are often more successful than efforts to raise money for homeless humans, even when all things are roughly equal.

I have often wondered whether too much empathy is worse than too little. Either way there's a "failure of feeling" as Wallace Stevens noted. Should the Bible's worthy plowman *never* look back? It's true that a backward glance or fond recollection might cause wrinkles in the farmer's furrows, but will the farm fail? Rose Kennedy thought that self-pity was fatal, but I've yet to see that in any coroner's report. It should be noted, however, that Mrs. Kennedy lived to be 104½. Like many symptoms, feeling sorry for yourself is treatable, but if you don't "explore every sensation of [your] soul," as Lord Byron said, who will?

William James thought the image of an Edwardian coachman and his client offered a succinct contrast between sentimentality and indifference. Inside a Brougham sits an aristocratic lady snug in her furs, weeping for "Little Nell," who'd died on stage just minutes earlier. Outside sits a poor coachman, feeling nothing but the cold rain running down his back. Inured to the hardships of his profession, the coachman is as incapable of tears for Nell as the lady is hardened to the man driving her home.

I find it interesting that this stoic coachman will scream for eleven footballers he's never met and perhaps even weep when they lose in the playoffs. But take this same bloke to see an early twentieth-century equivalent of *The Field of Dreams*, and he'll blubber like the woman in the cabin of his carriage. Unless, that is, he's wired like my father.

After his ninety-fifth birthday party at my sister's home in Tucson, it fell on me to drive Dad to the assisted-living facility that he now called home. He'd recently lost his driving privileges, which pleased everyone except our stoic widower. Given his failing health and abilities, we all knew that this was likely to be the last time we would celebrate anything with him. Dodging the potholes in Camino Real and mulling the bittersweet stories shared at the party, I wiped the tears with my sleeve. Uncomfortable with the silence, and attempting to alleviate what I perceived to be Dad's sadness, I asked him what was on his mind. With the evenness of a career bureaucrat, he said, "I gave the city a thousand dollars a year ago to pave this road." But then my military father had never been a sentimental man, lest feelings interfere with duty.

Reviewing some of the literature of emotion, I stumbled on the possibility that "maw" and "mawkish" may be etymological cousins. Indeed, the tide of sentiment, which has flooded the brain racing for the lachrymal flats, often has a sickly odor like chocolate in a dog's mouth. Commercially, those things I consider cornball include Las Vegas, shell sculptures, white lipstick, taxidermy, and fuzzy dice. Musically, they may take the form of Al Capone's "Madonna Mia." (Yes, that Al Capone.) Visually, they may resemble Walter Keane's mascara-eyed children that haunt the walls of K-Mart. And in poetry, they may be modelled on "Papa's Letter." These are verses by an anonymous Victorian who wrote, "Please, dear mama…I's tired of the kitty / want some ozzer fing to do. / Writing letters, is 'ou mama? / Tan't I wite a letter too?" If that strumming of the heart strings wasn't frothy enough, the author-mother glues a stamp on the boy's forehead and sends him off as a "letter" to his dead father. Returning from the post office that turned him away, the boy is trampled by a team of runaway horses. But the writer assures us that all is not lost, for "Papa's letter" has been delivered to heaven. Reading the entire poem may remind one of comedian Jim Sherbert's observation "that fifteen minutes into a Jerry Lewis telethon you start rooting for the disease?"

It is reported that Lenin once ordered a pianist who lived nearby to stop playing the "Appassionata," lest it weaken his revolutionary resolve. Given the failings of communism, perhaps he should have allowed Beethoven to work his magic.

Like the composer, emotionally mature writers risk sounding like a dishwasher's instruction manual if they don't appeal to sentiment. Likewise, for the rest, their hearts should also take the lead "since feeling is first" as E. E. Cummings reminds us. Running in second place, reason usually has a way of catching up, but whichever leads, I prefer the rue on rye. Hold the schmaltz.

Tried and Found Wanton: The Language of Sex

"The mad, white fish of the oval realm
often led me to ask, 'Who's at the helm?'
The stripes of my sail now droop at half mast
in luffing grief of a towering past." —*The Wordspinner*

So, exactly how do humans reproduce if we don't bifurcate, pupate, or molt? I'm glad the answer to the overwhelming question of my adolescence was not left entirely to my parents. Mother never said a word, which wasn't coded, on the subject, and Dad bought me a copy of *The Stork Didn't Bring You*, which he quietly left on my bedside table. Though it was the first and last book he ever bought me, it was never discussed and eventually passed along to my encrinolated sisters. Indeed, they had a code of their own: walking to Sunday school once, I overheard one tell the other, "It's snowing down south."

So at thirteen or fourteen, I turned to Mr. Randy Jackson, two years my younger but still ahead of the curve, who spoke to me of pistils and bees in the flowery language his parents had used. Mr. Neil Harte, who was my age, countered saying, "Navels are scars left by birth and proof that babies come from a woman's stomach." I didn't have the sense or courage to ask why the scars are so small or why some protrude and others don't. Nor did I ask how the pollen entered the stomach or why it wasn't digested. When I'd heard people use the word "womb," I thought they were mispronouncing "loom," but why anyone wanted to go back to one was a mystery.

The facts of life are not the sort of thing a boy asks his younger sisters about, especially after witnessing the following. My two sisters and I, all in our teens, were seated on the living room floor one Sunday scanning the comics and sports pages. Suddenly Mother entered from the laundry room waving a pair of panties and demanding, "Who fell off the roof?" My younger sister blushed, stammered an apology, cried, and ran from the room. Mother then sent the older to find her and instruct her in what I assumed were the basics of feminine hygiene. In seconds, she had doffed the mantle of responsibility and draped it over her older daughter.

Wanting to know but not wanting to know, I went along contentedly curious about these mysteries until I married, but my German wife didn't know much more than I did: it was my aunt, not Ingrid's mother, who introduced her to the vinegar douche. The stork book probably held more answers, but it was an ocean away.

Now fast forward to a family reunion when Mother, now seventy-five, mentioned a cream she'd bought for her arthritis. To illustrate its strength, she went to the bedroom for a jar of Equi-ment, whose label stated, "For race horses only…sold by trainers and veterinarians…active ingredient capsaicin, what makes hot peppers hot!" As my sisters, their husbands, my wife and I were dabbing this horse liniment on the backs of our hands, Mother said, "I use it on Daddy too when he's in the mood—he wears me out!" Dad, who was cutting a pie in the kitchen a few feet away, yelled, "Watch out, kids—this stuff produces the original hot rod!"

Long before I reached retirement age, I understood the veiled references above, but I also had acquired an interest in the rites and language of sex. I never wanted to be as ignorant as I was when Mother waved that pair of soiled panties before her three "blank slates." Though friends have told me I'm fortunate I didn't get the oral equivalent of oozing venereal sores they received, I still think I was short changed.

Many years later, I'm pleased to report that our sixteen-year-old grandson knows the difference between his Cowper's glands and his epididymis, while I, for all my years of word collecting, never knew I had either one. In a somewhat less technical field, however, I consider myself wiser than Tolstoy who thought "copulation an abomination." I come down on the side of the country versifier who said,

"A little coitus
Never hoit us."

❋

Though I'd been raised a Presbyterian, the very idea that we'd ever seriously entertained predestination left me in a spiritual tailspin. I began reading about Catholicism and discovered early church fathers like Tertullian, who'd taught that women were "temples" built over "sewers"; St. Jerome, who'd taught that the "too passionate husband is an adulterer," and St. Augustine, who'd taught that procreation is the only righteous reason for intimacy. Noting that two of these men had been canonized, I turned to Judaism and read that Rabbi Eliezer thought rich men were entitled to sex every day while camel drivers could sleep with their wives once a month. Offended by this failure of democracy, I turned to Islam, only to discover that the Ayatollah Khomeini had approved pedophilia and bestiality under certain conditions. Finally, in disgust, I decided the stork book had more to offer, so I located a reasonable facsimile and read it cover to cover.

On the subject of sex, my grandmother's advice

amounted to, "Don't canoddle in sin"; her poetic gardener advised "trellising desire"; my Latin teacher told a class, "Propinquity leads us to propink"; and King Lear, ranting on the moors, said, "Let copulation thrive." Recognizing that there's some truth in each of these, I finally decided that anything consenting adults do in private is fine with me. While turtles tup, hawks cawk, fish spawn, and bucks rut, humans are permitted all of the above, including "humming the castanets" and "consulting the hairy oracle."

Perhaps because football is more popular in the South than baseball, "gridiron speech" is the preferred creole "down home," especially when it comes to sex. Each side supplies its own "field judge," and whatever fans there are should not be allowed on the "playing field." As the game unfolds, "great hands" help to avoid "fumbling," but the play is as mental as it is physical; thus, one needs the "flexibility" to call an "audible." Foreplay consists of the "coin toss" followed by the "kickoff" though feet are rarely used to advance the ball. The receiving side then has several options to "run" or "pass." If that side fails to gain ten yards in three attempts, it's obliged to "punt." If the punter gets enough "hang time," he might pin the opposition in the "red zone." Occasionally one is sent "to the showers" for an "illegal procedure," but more often a player is just "sidelined." However, if enough first downs are made by either side without any "unnecessary roughness," and with the courage to "go deep," a "score" is likely. With any luck, the game will go into "overtime." Unlike football, however, sexual scoring should be mutually satisfying, leaving both sides smiling from the "contact."

※

In January of 2014, I read in *Harper's* that Texans are permitted to own as many guns as they wish but no more than five dildos. Clearly, values are not just changing, there's been a paradigm shift. Though it took nearly two thousand years to reach America's shores, my copy of the *Kamasutra* openly describes the "doe woman of Koshola" who's mastered the "Clasp of the Serpent," the "Kiss Palpitating," the "Half-Moon Scratch," and "Eating the Mango." In New York newspapers I find ads for strippers with stage names like Letha Weapons, Tawnie Peaks, Heidi Hooters, and Staci Staxxx. The poet W. H. Auden casually referred to his penis as a "giggle stick" and a woman's genitals as, "Fumbler's Hall." My mentor James Dickey once complained before a mix of undergraduates and graduates that intercourse with older women was as unsatisfying as "waving your arm in a warm room." A black student of my own told a class that her white boyfriend was "skinny but well-hung." Finally, the municipal recreation center that my wife and I use is currently advertising both a "booty boot camp" and "a bridal booty camp."

The days when professors would send the untenured to the pharmacy to buy condoms is thankfully past. Now both male and female condoms are given away in college dormitories and clinics with advice to "Wrap that rascal!" "Courting" college students are often urged to ask before making any romantic moves. "Do unto others," the Bible says, but first ask: "May I kiss you; may I unhook your bra; may I fondle your breasts...." When these guidelines were announced at Antioch College in 1993, they were widely mocked, but the erotic possibilities of this new language are endless.

And while it's still a good idea to "trellis desire," younger readers should be grateful they were born after the Agricultural, Industrial, and Sexual Revolutions.

From Elf Locks to Bed Hair: Slang

"If words form a spectrum, slang is infrared—
unseen but hot, it pokes the maidenhead." —*The Wordspinner*

"One day it's *hip*, the next it's *hep*—
you think you're cool but are a schlep." —*The Wordspinner*

Before my parents stopped smoking, two matching Ronson lighters weighed heavily on the end tables. Dad said he bought them after WWII to remind him of a friend who'd died in one of the tanks the troops nicknamed "Ronsons" because they were so susceptible to fire. In the Viet Nam War, the floating gas tanks that patrolled the Mekong Delta were nicknamed "Zippo boats" (after the famed military-issue lighters) by the men who sailed these boats for the same reason that tank crews had named their steel tombs.

"Ronson tanks" and "Zippo boats" embody some of the fatalism and grit that often make slang interesting to an acolyte of language. As Carl Sandburg said, "Slang is language that rolls up its sleeves, spits on its hands, and goes to work." In other words, slang is not generated behind a Pentagon desk; it's made in a Humvee on patrol in Baghdad. The brass straighten their ties and fabricate jargon like "manually powered fastener-driving impact devices" for hammers. GIs, on the other hand, spit on their hands and hammer out subversions like "BOHICA" for "bend over, here it comes again" and "African golf" for the crap games that enlisted men love to play.

Ambrose Bierce thought slang was "the speech of him who robs the literary garbage carts on the way to the dump." That description is far too cynical for a term like "teleruba," an allusively euphonious term for television. Raley Bell, on the other hand, thought slang was the "voice of the god that dwells in the people." If Bell is correct, how does one account for terms like "whistling beef," a synonym for vomiting? But if Bierce and Bell are off the mark, what is slang?

The word's etymology may offer some help. A few historians think "slang" was cobbled in the 1750s from five letters in the middle of "beggars' *lang*uage." Others speculate that it derived from a Norse phrase meaning to "sling the jaw." Both explanations seem over-ingenious, but I have nothing better. The usual dictionary definition reads something like this: informal or non-standard language. The problem is that one might say the same of dialect or creole.

One thing is certain: English speakers were using slang long before they had a word for it. Take sex: in 1351, Jack gave Jill a "green gown"; by 1505, this randy pair was playing "nug-nug"; in 1621, they received a "night physic"; in 1656, they "joined paunches"; in 1680 it was their "giblets" they joined; in 1863, they were enjoying a "horizontal refreshment," and in 1910 they were "having their ashes hauled." In 2016, it's everything from "sleep with" to "hook up" with many prudish to graphic variations in between. Perhaps thousands of other examples exist (I'm not counting), but a census brings us no closer to a definition. Thus, it may be more helpful to explore some of the more salient attributes of slang.

Stealing a botanical term, I used to tell students that slang is "the growth bud of language." Shifting the metaphor, it's linguistic yeast, a catalyst, or a new wave of immigrants. In other words, a "buttload" of slang may enter English and serve an apprenticeship before rising to journeyman or master's status. "Clever," "blizzard," and "fun," for example, entered English labeled "substandard," but over the years, all three rose to respectability. Occasionally, the opposite happens: "buttload of wine" in 1400 was a perfectly respectable measure of 108 imperial gallons. But as my quotations above around "buttload" indicate, this is not true today.

Sigmund Freud observed that the first man to hurl a curse instead of a stone was the father of civilization. Generally, men do create more slang than women: there are, for example, over three hundred terms to describe falling off a skateboard, and most of these were coined by teenage males. But even after ten thousand years of farming and living in towns, substituting slangy threats for violence remains a challenge. Indeed, ever since our cross-street neighbors moved in a couple of years ago, I have been tempted to "throw a stone." Instead, I've told everyone except our cross-street neighbors that I hate their "lawn mullet": a yard that's short and business-like up front, but shaggy in the back. Thus slang is compensatory, mocking an undeserved fate as it does, for I mow the front and back yards fifteen to twenty times a season.

Recently, a former colleague, who lives out of town, emailed me asking about a memorial service for a mutual friend. Rodney had been a navy pilot before he became an English professor, and I had served three years in the army, so I wrote him back saying the service was at "1900 Z." Though he arrived at 1915 Z, it was not my phrasing that caused him to be late; he'd gotten lost. My allusion to what the military calls "Zulu time" was a casual display of our "union card."

Another friend seems incapable of conducting a conversation without inserting a new medical slang term he's picked up in the ER where he volunteers. Subconsciously, he's using slang to mark the limits between him, an MD, and me, a PhD. In the course of one conversation, he said that "TMB" Joe was "GPO" and probably headed for the "ECU" following his latest "UBI." What he meant was: Too-many-birthdays Joe was good for parts only and probably headed to the eternal care unit following his latest unidentified beer injury. What my medical friend may not realize is that the on-line Urban Dictionary defines most of his slangy abbreviations, thus lowering the bar between us.

❀

As soon as "bootylicious" entered on-line dictionaries, it was sure to be followed by "boobalicicious," "nipplelicious, "hunkalicious," etc. Far more of these inflationary terms will depart the commonweal's vocabulary than remain, but some like "third-shift mosquito" for "lightning bug" and "bird sheriff" for "game warden" one can only hope will stay.

I've been a slangaphile longer than I've been a poker player, but I still don't know if "a pair of tits" is one queen or two. Whether one considers it "anti-language," "cryptolect," or just, "the poor man's language," slang has the undeniable power to stop mall Santas from saying "ho, ho, ho," force Beaver College to change its name to Arcadia University, and force the *New Yorker* to publish an explanation of "give great cubicle." Whatever this dark energy is, may its generative force remain strong, for the death of Latin slang was the death of that spoken language.

One Nation Divided by the Same Language: Black Slang

"[Slang is] the speech of him who robs the literary garbage carts on the way to the dumps." —*Ambrose Bierce*

"[Slang is] the voice of the god that dwells in the people." —*Raley Bell*

One night, Mack Daddy and Delores drove deep into the projects because, as Daddy said, "I wanna holla at my peeps. I promised Mamadukes a long time ago I'd never forget who brung me. Plus, we be rollin' on some phat deuce-zero dubs, and I wanna give my homies an eyeful of these kickin' spinners. I gave a week's worth of scratch for them, mind you, nothin' boojee. You feel me, Boo?"

"Aight, Mack Daddy, tru dat. I'm so iced out, I wanna troll the 'hood myownself. I ain't clownin'—I wanna show One-Eyed Wanda my baby's daddy and my hot ice. That 'hood rat don't know ice from bling. You cool beans with dat?"

Before Daddy could answer, a motorcycle officer rolled up from somewhere in the projects with his blue light on. "Slow ya roll, Mack Daddy," said the officer, "You look like you're ridin' dirty—ya don't mind if I nose around in your lunch, do ya?"

Said Daddy, "Dayum, What's a brother got to do to get some love around here?" As Daddy was emerging from his car, he said, "I know you ain't throwin' salt on my game, hossifer, so help yourself to my dirty draws. You know the 'hood ain't been good to me—I don't own a gat, I'm way low on ducketts, and I ain't scored a good weed in months. Now ax yourself, would I be all ragged out if I be dealin'? I don't think so. And fa' shizzle I wouldn't be havin' this dime piece with me if I was."

As the officer searched Mack Daddy's Accord, Wanda in hot-pink shorts stepped from the back door of an Escalade saying, "Wassup, playa?"

"Nuthin' much. I be chillin' like a villain," replied Mack Daddy. "What it is?"

"I don't know—I can't seem to get my ba-donk-a-donk in gear these days 'cause my laffy taffy ain't shakin' no mo'."

"That's a damn shame, Wanda, 'cause you always did have some fine cake. No one ever called you 'buttaface'— least while I was around."

"Thank you, Mack Daddy—you always be knowin' how to make a girl feel good about herself. Hit me on the hip sometimes," said Wanda with a wink of her good eye.

"Play your cards right, girl, and one night, we'll get your swirl on. What yo' digits?"

"Shut your grill and keep yo' plastic pants on, One-Eye," interrupted Delores, who'd been opening the trunk for the officer. "After my ex bust a cap in yo' butt two years ago, you lost all juice in the 'hood—now get back to yo' crumb snatchers, and leave my baby's daddy be."

"Cool it, Schawty—I don't want no drama on this bubblin' corner," said Daddy snapping his collar up.

"Aw, we just be jawsin'. My b," said Wanda apologetically. The last thing they heard her say as she walked off was, "Keep it real now, one love, and don't be crackin' on me."

Turning away, Mack Daddy said, "I wouldn't dis Wanda to her face, but dat girl is tow up from the flo' up."

Wondering whether she was a ghetto-fabulous dime or just another skoochie, Delores said, "Now if Sam the man is done searchin' yo' whip and jackin' our time, le's bounce."

Living with Uranus: Speech

"The tongue's a towel that strikes with a snap,
or lies in the locker after a flap." —*The Wordspinner*

"If this poet could speak, he would not write—
he'd find a soapbox to set things right." —*The Wordspinner*

Aunt Grace used to say that sugar can sweeten everything from salt to cyanide, but it won't stop either from killing you. She was referring to what Southerners call "sweet talk": the art of convincing a starving dog to drop his meaty bone, or as my Uncle Bob once said, a blend of "saccharine and bullshit." Grace unriddled the term when a divorced friend told her how much their friendship meant to her and then seduced her husband. My aunt was tempted to retaliate, but cancer claimed her before she could sweeten the rat poison.

I was reminded of the sweet talkin' woman who ran off with Bob recently reading of the Boston Marathon bomber. Dzhokhar Tsarnaev, the curly-headed nineteen-year-old who'd made the cover of *Rolling Stone*, was not the well assimilated immigrant most everyone thought he was. After killing four and injuring some 260, Tsarnaev's thick Chechen accent returned when he divulged his true colors.

It isn't so much "what we say" as "how we say it" that has been on my mind lately. A young fund raiser for my *alma mater* called recently asking if I was "Dr. Eisiminger, Emeritus." I've learned to live with the tortured mispronunciations of my surname, but I'd never heard "emeritus" pronounced "em-ur-**EYE**-tis" as if it were an ophthalmic infection.

Ever since I pronounced my father's beloved "Corps of Engineers" as the "Corpse of Engineers," I have been sympathetic to those who misspeak. As a corrective, Dad had me stand at attention and say "core of engineers" a hundred times. This was only half helpful because while I quickly mastered the pronunciation, I still had difficulty with the spelling. To this day, I think of the dam-building Corps as the core of the military.

Many mispronunciations like our son's "cham-uh-**LEE**-on" for "chameleon" persuade us to smile. Recently, I caught myself smiling at a second grader as she read to me at the school where I volunteer. The adventures of a "wimpy kid" were unfolding reasonably well until the reader arrived at "young." After I hinted, "yuh, yuh," she brightened and exclaimed, "Unicorn!" With little more than a passing glance, this child found a "rainbow" in "raise" and "potty paper" in "pretty paper." I know of no brain scan that lays bare the mind of a seven-year old as well as reading aloud.

Listening to an African-American second-grader one morning, I was reminded of the time I drove my wife to Emory for a checkup. While waiting in the lobby, I asked one of the hospital clerks as I pointed to a construction site, "Excuse me, but what are they building across the parking lot?"

"That's for the chiren," said a fiftyish black woman.

"The what?"

"The chiren's hospital," she said.

"What's a cheer-in hospital?" I wondered.

"No, no," a passing nurse said laughing, "that's the new children's hospital." I laughed too, as did the clerk who proudly refused to be thrown off of her dialectal stride. As they say in the broadcast booth, "No harm, no foul."

The colleague, who taught me that sporting expression, once vowed that he could help an African-American sophomore pronounce "ask" without a reference to what he called, "crude forest tools." Said the professor to the student in the privacy of his chambers, "Say 'ass' for me."

"Ass."

"Good. Now say it again with a 'k' on the end."

"Axe."

It's true that word may have been pronounced "aks" in Chaucer's day, but you won't hear Barack Obama say it. I've read that some Tiger Korean parents have the vertical flap of skin beneath the tongue surgically cut to help their children pronounce the English "r." Before I did something that extreme, I'd learn to live with "flied lice."

Jerry Seinfeld has observed that many people attending a funeral would rather be the deceased than the eulogist. I know that when I have spoken on those sad occasions the words seemed to converge like buses at the mouth of the Lincoln Tunnel: thirteen lanes funneling into four. It seems that grief mixed with embarrassment is a potent deterrent to public speaking. When we're obligated to speak beside a fresh grave, articulation is that much more difficult.

My wife Ingrid and I know an elderly kvetch who claims to have kissed the Blarney Stone on a trip to Ireland. She must have French kissed it because often she has more mouth than geese have hind quarters. Anyway, she cornered Ingrid recently as she was climbing from the recreation-center pool. Sensing what was in store, Ingrid excused herself saying she was going to use the sauna before showering and dressing. To her astonishment, the fully dressed woman followed her into the cedar chest where the temperature was just below that at which blood boils. Whether it was the heat or the humidity, her story of adolescent hook-ups alternated between "bi-ligamists" and "poly-bigamists."

Some vocalizations like the "Northern European puff" defy mispronunciation. I say "Northern European" because I have only heard it used by Germans and Norwegians, but it may well be universal. To illustrate, imagine you are being scolded by a German visitor for the infamy of our gun crimes. Then you say, "But real gun-law reform is impossible as long as the Second Amendment is in place."

"Pff," says your visitor with a barely audible puff of disdain before launching into a discourse on America's decline.

It's remarkable that despite radio, television, and the internet there's really no McEnglish despite the fact that most cross-country truckers sound alike. Nevertheless, as the punch line goes, any word uttered with a foreign accent may be held against you. I remember a bias I held against a British professor of history who pronounced "bomb" as "bum." Even though I couldn't find any other weaknesses, I could not forgive him—until he gave me the grade I was hoping for.

Regardless of history, accent, or dialect, it pays to research an audience. Some political analysts say John Kerry lost Nevada in 2004 when he repeatedly referred to the state as "Nuh-**VAH**-duh" instead of "Nuh-**VAD**-uh."

※

Voltaire was annoyed that "ague" was spoken with two syllables while "plague" had only one. Some of us call the seventh planet from the Sun: ur-**ANUS**, while others say: **UR**-in-ous. Either way, the result is an unearthly blend. The richness (and rankness) of our language and the endless variations we weave with the muscles of our mouths is one more reason we never grow tired of studying it. Perhaps this is why humanities professors use four times as many "uhs" in their lectures as their colleagues in math and science: language is simply more complex and, dare I say it, interesting.

Help! Help! Tautologies

"I have made this letter longer than usual because I lack the time to make it short." —*Blaise Pascal*

"Less is more." —*Robert Browning*

Tautologies are brief, usually clichéd redundancies like "safe haven" or "tuna fish." These two are redundant because by definition, havens are safe places, and tuna are fish. Metaphorically speaking, a tautology is formed when two acorns fall in the same hole, take root, and produce a single tree. Realistically, ignorance is the origin because beginning writers, unsure of a word's meaning, often add another they know rather than open a dictionary. Many tautologies have legal origins because lawyers often feel they need to repeat themselves to clarify or emphasize a point. But on closer inspection, such repetition in most written or spoken discourse is like dotting an "i" or crossing a "t" twice; it's unnecessary. As my high school English teacher used to say: "The death of the superfluous is unmourned."

With all tautologies italicized in the paragraphs below, I hope to prove my point, however, some examples are more egregious than others.

Full of *vim and vigor*, Lord Barton of Barton skipped out the door, looking at the walls of his estate, which had fallen to *rack and ruin*. All his servants gone, no longer a soul at his *beck and call*, Barton was forced to drive himself down the *highways and byways* to town. As he crossed the tracks into the factory district, he encountered a *wild and woolly* scene of scuffling workers, perhaps a *hue and cry* against the recent layoffs at Barton, Ltd.

Ever *hale and hearty*, Barton stopped his car and cried,

"*Cease and desist*! *Lo and behold*, in this *day and age*, filled though it is with *trials and tribulations*, we must be all the more *bound and determined* to *forgive and forget*. Let us do *anything and everything* to achieve *peace and quiet*. The *whys and wherefores* of our problems have *prim and proper ways and means* to deal with them. It is *well and good* that we *hem and haw* about what is *first and foremost* as we *pick and choose*. The *various and sundry* solutions, I believe, are *one and the same*, *part and parcel* of our destiny. So let's focus our *might and main* on the whole *kit and caboodle* as we work together."

The effect of this plea on the workers was *null and void*.

'Pro Bozo Publico' and Other Bilingual Tales: Translation

"If she's beautiful, she's unfaithful; if she's faithful, she's ugly." — *Voltaire*

"A perfect translation is impossible yet absolutely necessary." — *Anonymous*

Cervantes compared the translation of a classic to the backside of a tapestry: pale, dusty and knotted. Indeed, the difference between the original and the imitation may be as striking as "toadstool" and "Mr. Toad's stool." I recall observing a foreign tourist at Pizza Hut who wanted mushrooms on his pie. Unable to recall the English word for the topping he desired, he took out his pocket Hexaglot, struck a few keys, and asked the counter clerk for "a medium, thin-crust pizza with fungi." Chuckling at the end of the line, I was reminded of Evelyn Waugh's observation, "No man who knows more than one language can express himself memorably in any."

A single-panel cartoon by Mark O'Donnell in *Spy Magazine* captured some of Waugh's sentiments. In a characterless café, a translator is having a drink with a writer whose back is turned. Says the translator, "Do you not be happy with me as the translator of the books of you?"

Married to a German woman for fifty-three years, I have acquired some modest experience translating from one language to another. I also have forty-two years' experience teaching native English speakers how to communicate in Standard Written English. Far too often, the latter practice is like teaching Pashtun to pumpkins. Prodding eighteen-year old students with a passable command of the colloquial to a level of English that will make them employable, I have come to appreciate the difficulties of preserving the rhythms, humor, and connotative complexity of the speech they bring to the classroom. Often, however, much is lost in the "translation" of the students, the result of which is ignorance in two "languages."

Frankly, the majority of Americans do not need a second language; they need a finer control of the one they absorbed through osmosis. As Emerson is reported to have said, "Why should I swim the Charles River when there's a bridge?" Or as I used to say when studying Latin in high school, "Why am I wasting my time parsing verbs when there are translations of Cicero in the library?" Frankly, I believe there's more to be gained from reading those translations than learning the correct usage of *amas* and *amat*. Winston Churchill, incidentally, agreed with me, and he won the Nobel Prize for Literature as well as a world war. Yes, there's a certain mental discipline gained from studying Latin and calculus, but the majority of students I've taught will find English and business math more useful and satisfying.

At the risk of sounding like a snob, let me tell you of an encounter with the Catholic custodian who used to clean the offices and classrooms in the building where I once taught. A parochial school graduate with a semester of Spanish, Philip was, nevertheless, a man of suboptimal intelligence, but he had the street smarts that permitted him to hold a job when others were collecting welfare. One day with a few minutes to kill before class, I saw him mopping the hall outside my office near the men's room. Seeking to engage him in some friendly banter, I said, "Hey, Philip. I see you have a new sign."

"No, I've been using this yellow-plastic thingy for a couple of months."

"I'm surprised I never noticed it because this one is interesting," I said brightly. "See, it says 'closed' in German, French, Spanish, and English."

"I reckon English is plenty for me," Philip said, "but on the floors below, the kids might could use these other words."

"You mean in the language department?"

"Yeah."

"Well, if some ignoramus doesn't understand these," I noted, "there's this open-hand symbol here."

"What's the hand mean?"

"Duh—'*closed*.'"

If I'd worked a physically demanding job or jobs like Philip for forty years, I probably wouldn't know that *geschlossen* means "closed" in German either. Frankly I was just guessing at the Spanish, but I didn't tell Philip that—I was too embarrassed by the horse-Protestant way I'd treated him.

As long as there are six languages spoken at the United Nations, eleven in the European Union, and 7,358 across the globe, there will be translators, for they *are* useful. With a decent translation of the Old Testament, Michelangelo would not have carved horns on Moses's head. With a translator who understood the subtleties of the Japanese word *mokusatsu*, President Truman may never have ordered the atomic bombs on Hiroshima and Nagasaki. And if we ever get a Qur'an with "seventy-two virgins" translated as "seventy-two white raisins," we may find fewer young men willing to blow themselves up in a Jerusalem marketplace.

Where, I often wonder when our president is abroad, is St. Jerome's lion to sic on errant translators? Where was a good State Department interpreter when Jimmy Carter

said, "I to want to know the Polish people carnally," or when John Kennedy announced in Berlin that he was a "jelly doughnut"? The problem often lies with consecutive translation. Instead of waiting for a speaker to finish a statement and letting a translator read a consensus, the underpaid assistant often begins work on a sentence before the speaker has reached the verb nestled at the end. Needless to say, this practice is often dangerous, but it happens almost every day at the UN.

Translating any oral text is a bit like Telephone, the party game in which the message spoken at the end seldom resembles the whispered input. Perhaps no translation is more controversial than the English Bible which has roots in Hebrew, Aramaic, and pidgin Greek, two of which are no longer spoken by anyone except a few specialists. Depending on the scholar you read, the Bible was orally transmitted for one hundred to a thousand years. Serious readers of the Bible, therefore, should take the approach that the Rev. Franklin Graham reportedly took with President George W. Bush. When Bush asked the minister about the off chance of the meek inheriting the earth, Graham assured the president that the famed beatitude is a mistranslation. Indeed, if *meek* is understood as "humbly self-confident," the prophecy has already come true in much of the world. Bible Gateway, an on-line comparison of twenty-two English translations, reveals that we really don't know how to translate *meek* because it has been rendered variously as "gentle," "content," "mild," "patient," "long-suffering," "humble," "mournful," and "trusting." No one translates *meek* as "submissive," but I'd be willing to bet that's the way most Americans like the ex-president understand it.

Unless a life is at stake and despite all I've said above, I would change little in the majority of inept translations and writings of those whose first language is not English. I realized that recently reading through some old letters from a former student, who has returned to her native Taiwan to teach art. In 1994, Echo wrote to say that she was considering returning to the States to study English in "the Collage of Literal Arts." A pregnancy and her father's illness, however, changed those plans, and in 1995, she wrote fondly of the "Humanity" class she took from me. At Christmas in 2002, she wrote "for the great season and Holy Day." She closed her card saying, "Time is flying, and my life space is so limited. Few words but represent our deepest mind."

I wouldn't change a syllable.

Boiling the Lance: Recreational Linguistics

"The phrase 'to poach an egg' angered Eugene,
for words should mean one thing, not umpteen." —*The Wordspinner*

"'Fat chance' and 'slim chance' mean the same thing,
for in the Queen's English the jester is king." —*The Wordspinner*

In some old film whose title I have conveniently forgotten, a leading man told his leading lady that her face made time stand still. She tenderly kissed him; the director faded to black, and that was the end of it. As I often did, I tried to memorize smooth one-liners when I found them because uncertain as I was at twelve, I suspected I would need some poetic backup one day. However, when the time for help came, that one-liner emerged as, "Your face would stop a clock," and that too was the end of it.

Critical actions often hinge on arranging the right words in the right order—err on either count, and you may have your face slapped. I recall underscoring that paragraph in which Holden Caulfield mishears Robert Burns' line about "comin' through the rye" as "catcher in the rye" and how that mondegreen changed his life. Having been ridiculed in kindergarten after "I led the pigeons to the flag," I concluded like Holden that I'd better start paying closer attention to words.

To help in that effort, my father bought me a leather-bound, vest-pocket dictionary. It was here that I found "avuncular"while writing about the uncle who'd let me borrow his car, but when I looked for its equivalent to describe a benevolent aunt, I drew a blank. So I created "avantular," and my English teacher apparently read right past it.

Coining words was not only useful, I discovered, but fun, and after college, I drifted into a sky-blue, unfunded, subset of recreational linguistics, or "rec ling." When I thought I'd coined "objectifyingly" in the sentence, "Stone, a descendant of Medusa, could not help but look objectifyingly at women," I realized that I had a word unlisted in any of my print dictionaries. (On-line, I've since discovered that it's been used over nine hundred times.) But the more interesting feature for me was that here was a word with three suffixes! I felt like one of those savants who discover prime numbers surfing the waves of their cerebral seas. Actually, the feeling was more like that of the California owner of the Yreka Bakery when he realized he'd been given a palindrome without asking.

The next move was to see how many prefixes I could add to some impoverished stem. Some student of Greek had beaten me to "penultimate," meaning next to the last, but what if you wanted to call someone's attention to the sixth to the last item in a series? And thus was born "pro-supra-pre-ante-pen-ultimate." (Ordinarily, I don't use the hyphens, but I wanted to show where the fusions occurred.) Years later, a web search showed to my horror and admiration that someone had coined "supra-fore-pro-pre-ante-pen-ultimate," for the seventh item in a series. In the comments section of the creator's web page, a jealous rival had proclaimed it, "the worthless word of the day." I beg to differ.

One of our grandsons has apparently inherited the word gene from me. When Spencer was thirteen, he asked me if I knew the longest word in English. I said, "I'm pretty sure I do, but what do you think it is?" "Hippopoto-monstro-sesqui-pedalio-phobia," he chuckled. I didn't have the heart to tell him about "pneumo-ultra-micro-scopic-silico-volcano-coni-osis" or the little train station in Wales with the name that is almost as long as the trains that stop there. But his joy was undiminished when I told him about "smiles," a word whose start and finish are separated by an orthographic "mile."

One day, daydreaming over my keyboard, I noticed that while "sinister" requires two hands to type on QWERTY, "dexter"(right) is typed with the left alone. A Google search showed I was not in virgin territory wherein no hand had stepped. Some anonymous logophiles had determined that "stewardesses" is the longest word in modern English typed exclusively with the left hand, and "lollipop" is the longest using the right. "Typewriter" is the longest using the top row, and "skepticism" is the longest alternating using left and right. As for words that are neatly laid out for you by QWERTY, there's "we" and "as," while pre-spelled names include "Io" and "Ty." The record for the middle row is "Shakalshas," a group of Turkish emigres living in Sicily. Unless one accepts "zzz" as a synonym for "sleeping" or "xxx" meaning "pornographic," I've yet to discover a word, not an acronym or abbreviation, which might be constructed from ZXCVBNM, the bottom row.

My favorite and largest category, however, is the superlative, which includes words fixed at the apogee or nadir of their orbits. These include in no particular order:

- The largest Roman-numeral word: "mix" (1009)
- The longest word that does not use "a," "e," "i," "o," or "u": "rhythms"
- My most beautiful word: "asphodel" (Who knew there were flowers in hell?)
- The least expected demonym: "Leodensian" (a resident of Leeds, UK)

- My proudest crossword clue: "elbows on the table" (pasta)
- My hardest word to pronounce: "isthmus" (I hesitate every time I say it.)
- The strongest denial: "I ain't never seen no such thing, no how, no way." (a quintuple negative)
- The longest word with 180° rotational symmetry: "SWIMS"
- My hardest tongue twister: "The sixth sick sheik's sixth sheep's sick."
- My sexiest word: "lubricious"
- The most often confused words: "its" and "it's" ("Their," "there," and "they're" run a close second.)
- The most toxic word: the "n-word" (Even buried in this list and spelled euphemistically, it is the verbal equivalent of plutonium. It may be the one word Donald Trump won't use.)
- The most disgusting word: "smegma" (the cheesy secretion beneath an unwashed foreskin)
- The best word without a vowel: "cwm" (a mountain lake and/or its steep-walled valley)
- The best word without a consonant: "Iouea" (a Cretaceous sponge)
- The most dangerous word: "inflammable" (It can mean both "not flammable" and "very flammable.")
- The longest word in alphabetical order: "abillowy" (I claim credit for adding the "a.")
- The longest one-syllable word: "squirrelled" (UK spelling)
- The best visual words: "Bed" and "bed" (The first has a fluffy pillow.)
- The shortest word with the most syllables: "etui" (I pronounce it with three syllables despite what the

French say.)

- The longest single word palindrome: "kinnikinnik" (an Alaskan shrub)
- The best synonym for "synonym": "equivalent"
- Longest reflection grouping: "X88B88" (voodoo)
- Longest snowball sentence: "I do not know where family doctors acquired illegibly perplexing handwriting; nevertheless, extraordinary pharmaceutical intellectuality, counterbalancing indecipherability, transcendentalizes intercommunications' incomprehensibleness." (lil thugsta)
- Longest set of homonyms: "raise, rays, rase, raze, rehs, réis, res"
- Shortest word with all six vowels in alphabetical order: "facetiously"
- The sole honest number: "four" (four letters that mean "4")
- The best oxymoron: "oxymoron" (the Greek roots are "sharp" and "dull")
- The eeriest anagram: "the meaning of life"/"the fine game of nil"
- Rich Hall's finest sniglet: "potentater" (the longest French fry in any order of fries)
- The longest word without a repeated letter: "uncopyrightables"
- The funniest malapropism: "After Skip's prostate surgery, he was incompetent."
- The longest kangaroo word and its joey: "municipality" and "city"
- The most widely understood English slang word: "okay" or "OK"

We've come a long way since "bankrupt" was spelled

"b-----pt" so as not to frighten readers of financial papers in 1900. But the freedom we enjoy in the twenty-first century has led some of my colleagues in "rec ling" to venture beyond the sign at the lip of the precipice: "Know Hope: One Way." I'm thinking of Cory Abbott who in 2012 transliterated *Alice in Wonderland* into alphagrams in which each of Lewis Carroll's words is reset in alphabetical order. Thus the title becomes: *Aceil in addelnnorW*. Cory Abbott, whose names are alphagrams, is rumored to be recuperating in the Henry Ford Center.

About the Author

Born December 12, 1941 at Walter Reed Hospital in Washington, DC, Skip Eisiminger is the son of Dorothy and Sterling Eisiminger. In 1959, he graduated from Mt. Vernon HS (his tenth school in twelve years). In 1963 while serving three and a half years in the Army Security Agency, he married Ingrid Barmwater of Helmstedt, West Germany. With her committed assistance, he graduated from Auburn University in 1967 (BS) and 1968 (MA). The same year, he settled his family in Clemson, SC after taking a job teaching English and interdisciplinary humanities at Clemson University. After his son Shane was born in 1964 and his daughter Anja in 1969, he returned to graduate school in 1970. In 1974, he graduated from the University of South Carolina with a PhD in English after which he returned to Clemson, where he looked forward to most Mondays until his retirement in 2010. His only move after his return was across town. Over forty-two years in academe, he published a book of verse, a book of word games, a children's book, and two collections of essays. In forty-two years as a teacher at Clemson, he taught over nine thousand students in twenty-nine different courses.

A recovering Presbyterian, Skip's firmest belief is in the illusion of free will. As a poet, he's aware rime does not pay; as an essayist, he knows it's not the eloquence but the evidence; as a critic, he assumes the best until he knows otherwise; as a linguist, he prides himself on being an ento-etymologist (a debugger of words); as a teacher, he has discovered if he makes the material seductive, the students will teach themselves; as an employee, he usually completed the worst first; as a husband, he comes to the table with something to share, and as a father and grandfather, he is a carpet bonder. Gradually, he has come to understand the virtue of giving more and expecting less, and that while curiosity did kill the cat, he has several more.